GWEN HEDLEY

SURFACES *FOR* STITCH

plastics • films • fabric

B T Batsford • London

ACKNOWLEDGEMENTS

My thanks go firstly to my husband Richard, whose unfailing support and
encouragement make all things possible.

Thanks also to embroidery students who over the years have urged me to go
into print – without their prodding, this book would never have been started.

Thank you to Michael Wicks, not only for his superb photography, but also his
forbearance and kind reassurances.

Lastly, but importantly, thank you to my friends who have shown interest and
been willing to listen and to comment, contributing much valued opinions.

First published 2000 by B T Batsford Ltd,

9 Blenheim Court

Brewery Road

London N7 9NT

A member of the Chrysalis Group plc

Text and designs © Gwen Hedley 2000

Photography by Michael Wicks

ISBN 0 7134 8666 X

Printed and bound in Spain by Bookprint, S.L., Barcelona

CONTENTS

INTRODUCTION

A few decades ago, embroidery was seen largely as a leisure craft, with a bias towards the decoration of household linens and garments. Commercially produced outline designs on paper were ironed on to fabric, and then embroidered in a variety of traditional stitches.

How the scene has changed! We still transfer designs to cloth, but the designs are generated by the embroiderer, using brushes, pens and dyes, with widely varying methods of transfer. Many of the traditional stitches are still employed, but with great freedom in terms of size and structure and the threads used. The sewing machine has become a tool for 'drawing and painting with thread', and the surfaces upon which we embroider can include tissue paper, polythene carrier bags or even potato sacks.

In selecting a surface for stitch, we must bear in mind the design source, for embroidery is not always a merely decorative art, concerned with reproducing a literal image. It can be a way of expressing ideas and impressions, and is increasingly considered as an interpretative art form. This is where the workbook comes into play. The committed embroiderer will, as a matter of course, carry a small notebook, for you never know when and where inspiration will strike. We are surrounded with ideas for design sources in our ordinary everyday environments. Rooftops and railings, plants and pebbles, hinges and handles, for example, can all provide new ideas for design. Observations should be recorded in your trusty notebook – not in the form of magnificent drawings, but in quick lines, sketches and words that describe colour and form. Look with intent at your design source, and try to capture its essence.

In observing and jotting down in words and/or pictures the characteristics of a subject, you will build a detailed knowledge of the source material, and a clear idea of the type of surface that will most accurately reflect it. The surface required for a stitched interpretation of water and ice will differ from that needed for mosses and lichens, and will demand different materials and approaches. Your notebook observations will tell you the nature of the surfaces required, and this book will hopefully guide you towards creating some of them.

This is a book about 'surface quality' rather than finished pieces, although the project section offers suggestions for using some of your stitched samples effectively. By increasing your awareness of the vast range of surfaces that it is possible to create, this book aims to encourage experimentation with a wide range of media and a full exploration of techniques. Hopefully, you will find that your approach to interpretative stitchery will be broadened and your work will become more adventurous. Above all, I hope that it will increase your enthusiasm for working with new and experimental surfaces, and promote the pleasures of creative stitching.

WORKING WITH THIS BOOK

Firstly, it is a good idea to familiarize yourself with the book. Get to know the layout and the approaches, and see the 'big picture' before you begin to home in on the detail.

When this book was planned, it was seen as a form of 'surface recipe book' into which the embroiderer might dip, in order to find an appropriate surface, alongside the recipe for creating it. However, just as the creative cook adds his or her own flavour and style to a standard recipe, so the artistic embroiderer will add his or her own touches to these. There are also suggestions for extending techniques and skills, which can make the work more personal to you.

The focus of the book is surface quality, and the key activities are experimenting and noting. You will need a workbook for notes and stitched samples. Spirally bound books, which expand to accommodate work, are ideal. Make detailed notes of your successes and failures (for you will have both), and jot down ideas and observations as they occur. You may think that you will remember how you did something, or why a sample didn't work, but in a few weeks' time, your memory could well fail you.

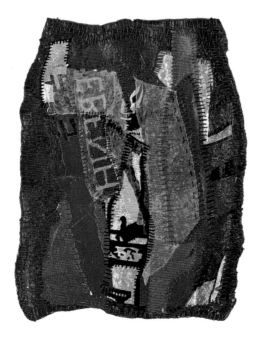

Do not have too set an idea of the outcome of experimental pieces, but work with an open mind. Capitalize on unexpected results, and look for the potential in any surface that you create. Take the 'what if... ?' approach to work. What if I do one or more of the following:

- paint it, then stitch again?
- cut it up and reassemble it?
- combine it with other materials?
- use it 3-dimensionally?
- work it on a different scale?
- layer it with other pieces?

In this way, you will create pieces that are truly your own, and build a source book full of interesting and challenging surfaces for stitch.

A word of warning – quick, slick effects can be very seductive! Remember that experimental activities are great fun, but are a step on the way and not an end in themselves. Always ask yourself whether the results reflect the nature of your inspiration. Ensure that the surface quality is sympathetic with and appropriate to the design source, and remember to follow design principles, considering balance of tone, texture, colour, line and form. Remember that unless they are used sensitively, many surface effects are obvious. Applied surfaces should be blended into the ground fabric with stitch and perhaps with colour, so that they are harmoniously integrated, avoiding jarring edges (unless such edges are part of the design).

Use this book as a working document, and the ideas in it as starting points for exciting stitch trials. Above all, use it with pleasure and a sense of adventure, charting your discoveries and plotting challenging paths forward.

Chapter One
Materials and Equipment

  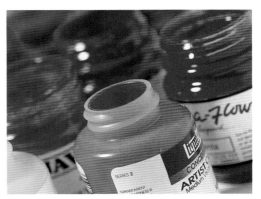

Innumerable pieces of equipment and many wonderful materials are available to us for use in embroidery today, but this section is limited to looking only at those used within this book. It is not always necessary to spend lots of money on specialist equipment, for it is often possible to use what we already have, or – with the aid of a little creative thinking – to make something similar.

COLOURING MATERIALS

While fabrics are readily available to us in a wide array of colours and designs, it is usually better to colour our own. In so doing, we are able to select the colours and designs that are most sympathetic to the work. Most of the plastics and films used here require surface colouring. Not all colouring agents can be used on any surface, so read the labels and carry out small trials if in doubt.

Drawing tools

Ordinary felt pens, crayons, coloured pencils and inks are all useful. They can safely be heated, and have the advantage of being readily and cheaply available.

Acrylic paints

These are particularly useful. Acrylic paints come in a multitude of colours and shades, including many attractive metallic and iridescent finishes, and are sold in tubes and jars. The consistency varies from free-flowing to buttery. Some brands, such as Liquitex Concentrate, come in easily manageable polythene jars with flip-top lids.

These paints are suitable for almost any surface; they can be thinned with water to any required

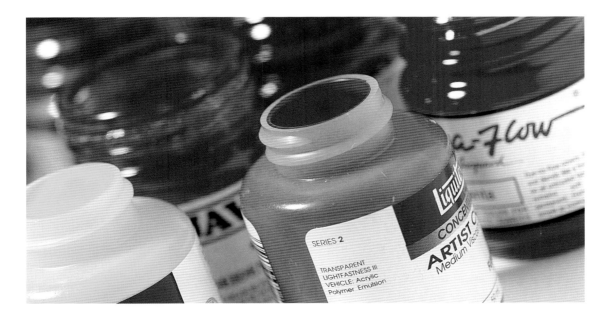

consistency, and they dry to a durable and flexible finish. They can be used on fabric, and do not need fixing. Diluting acrylics slightly with water reduces any subsequent stiffness in the fabric.

Fabric paints

As the name suggests, these are formulated for use on fabrics. Heat is used to set the colour and make it permanent on the cloth, paper, Tyvek, or other painted surface. Fabric paints can be either spirit- or water-based. Those used in this book are water-based paints, which are low in odour and safer for use in enclosed spaces.

Metallic powders

Also known as bronze powders, these are mixed with the appropriate binder to produce wonderfully rich metallic finishes, which are generally superior to those from ready-mixed metallic fabric paints. The powders are available in a wide range of golds, coppers and silvers, which can be mixed together for an even broader spectrum of metallics. The other advantage of

mixing your own metallic paints is the facility for varying the intensity of the metallic finish. Use just a little powder to give a mere hint of metal or large amounts for a heavy metallic gleam. Always wear a mask when handling powders, to avoid inhaling them.

Binders

Metallic binder (bronze binder) is the medium into which the metallic powders are mixed in order to make fabric paint, which is fixed by ironing. It is white, but dries to a transparent finish, revealing the full gleam of the metal powders. It can be diluted with water, so it is possible to apply a thin metallic wash. Varying amounts of ordinary non-metallic fabric paint can be added to the mixed metallic paint, to produce, for example, a red paint with a hint of gold to it, or conversely, a gold paint with a hint of red. Pearl binder can be used in the same way as metallic binder, to give a pearlescent finish.

Spray paints

These offer a quick and effective way of applying fine,

even coats of colour. Interesting and attractive tonal qualities can be achieved by applying sparse layers of several colours. Car spray paint is often used for art work, but there are hazards in this, especially if the process involves heating, as fumes may be produced. Some spray paints have been expressly designed for textiles, and florists' spray paints can also prove useful, so look around for suitable types. Read the sides of the can carefully before spraying, and always wear a protective mask when working with spray paint.

Silk paints

Although designed especially for silk, these can be applied to other fabrics and to paper. On fabric, these water-based paints are usually set with heat from an iron. They are very fluid and have a wonderful intensity and clarity of colour. Admittedly, the colours are at their most radiant when applied to pure silk, though a beautiful clarity is achieved on Tyvek.

TOOLS FOR APPLYING COLOUR

The implements used to apply colour will determine the marks and effects achieved, and it is advisable to have as wide a range of colouring tools as possible. Brushes are the most commonly used tools for applying paint, and their types are many and varied. Miscellaneous items, such as old knives, spatulas, spoons, plastic glue spreaders and small syringes, all have their uses, so keep a 'handy bag'.

Household brushes

Various widths and types of ordinary household brush are ideal for colouring large areas, and leave large-scale interesting brush marks in the surface.

Artists' brushes

It is advisable to buy a few good-quality artists' brushes. These must be well cared for, and not left neglected after use. Fine-pointed tipped brushes, flat wedge-ended, fan-shaped, and fat mop-ended brushes all give different effects and are worth trying out.

Stencilling brushes

These have densely packed short stiff bristles, and are the best type to use for accurate stippling and stencilling.

Toothbrushes

Old toothbrushes are particularly useful additions to the brush pot. They are excellent for splattering, and for rubbing paint into surfaces. They are also good to use for applying shoe polish and other coloured waxes to textured or irregular surfaces.

Cotton wool buds

These can be dipped into either paints or inks and used as drawing and colouring tools, to give lovely soft lines of varying intensity. You can also use them as print sticks, dabbing them down to give round soft dots of colour, which can be scattered or clustered. The dots get bigger as the tip wears out, so have a plentiful supply.

Sponges

Sponges are available in all sorts of shapes, sizes and textures, and make superb paint applicators. They can be used wet or dry, depending on the effect required.

Natural sponges

Small pieces of natural sponge, as sold at cosmetics counters, are ideal in size and shape. They can be used to dab paint on to a surface, giving their characteristic open, cellular design to each print. Overprinting can produce anything from a sparse to a totally dense covering of colour.

Synthetic sponge

Offcuts of synthetic sponge, either free of charge or costing very little, can often be obtained from upholsterers' workshops. These odd-shaped pieces are handy for cutting into other shapes, and will give a different finish to the natural sponge. Dragging creates a good streaked effect, while dabbing gives attractive areas with soft edges and varying colour concentrations.

Packing sponges from the tops of tablet jars, vitamin bottles and so on are usually circular, and make ideal print blocks. Push a cocktail stick through the middle to create a roller with which to apply narrow lines of colour.

Sponge brushes, available in a range of widths and lengths, produce a different effect from bristle brushes.

Sponge rollers provide a quick and effective way of covering areas, and are also excellent for applying paint to print blocks.

PRINTING OR STAMPING BLOCKS

These provide a quick and easy way to transfer a design to a surface. The design on the block can be printed in a regular pattern, as a border, as a single motif or quite randomly as an all-over abstract design. These useful pieces of equipment can often be made easily and cheaply from simple materials.

Wooden printing blocks

Readily available from many craft suppliers, these are generally imported from India. The design often features a bird or animal or, most usefully, a simple geometric motif. The latter are a valuable asset to your art store, as you can generally create different shapes and designs from the same block, depending on the orientation of each print.

Rubber stamps

These are also commercially available, but can easily be made. All you need is an eraser, which you cut with a craft knife to your chosen design. You can then glue the stamp to a small wooden block, using strong adhesive. Available from craft suppliers and even easier to use is the Speedy Stamp. This is a slab of easily cut pink rubber.

Softsculpt patches

Patches made from Softsculpt (see page 8) are very useful for printing line, motif and texture.

Card blocks

These are made by applying cut areas of thick card to a block of wood or a piece of heavy card, using strong glue.

String blocks

Blocks patterned with string are useful for printing designs composed of fine lines. The string must be sufficiently robust and firm to be glued to a wood block with a strong adhesive. For a short-lived block, secure the string with double-sided tape.

Sponge blocks

Carved sponge blocks give a wonderfully irregular

effect. The design is drawn on the sponge, then cut with scissors or a craft knife. If the sponge is of sufficient depth, it is not necessary to put it on a block, and the subsequent printing is subject to irregular pressure, giving subtle broken lines and soft-edged designs.

Other printing tools

Virtually anything can be used for printing – forks, corks, combs, cotton reels and pieces of card, for example – so a general odds and ends pot is always handy.

CUTTING TOOLS

It is very important to have the right tools for cutting, not only from the safety point of view, but also for accuracy and the quality of cut edges, and it is helpful to have a selection to use for specific purposes. Scissors and knives must be sharp, and it is worth being strict about keeping them in good condition.

Dressmaking scissors

These should be used only for cutting fabric; do not be tempted to use them for paper, as they will blunt quickly.

Embroidery scissors

Designed for snipping threads and neatening work, these are small and have pointed ends.

Lace scissors

These are even smaller than embroidery scissors, one blade being pointed and the other rounded, making it easy to pick up single threads and cut into fine areas without snagging other threads. These scissors are particularly good for cutting into layers of work.

Kitchen scissors

A pair of heavy-duty kitchen scissors is a useful, all-purpose tool for cutting sticks, metals, heavy plastics and so on.

Craft knives

Craft knives are ideal for cutting thick materials, such as card or heavyweight Vilene. They are also the best tools for cutting paper, or any material which requires a perfectly straight cut. The retractable and disposable blades are exceptionally sharp, and safety measures must be observed at all times. They should always be used with a metal safety ruler.

Metal safety ruler

This has a raised centre with a recess for the fingers.

Cutting boards

It is essential to work on a cutting board when using a craft knife. The best boards are the type that are flexible and 'self-healing', so that cuts in the surface of the board simply seal up again. These often have the advantage of being patterned with measuring grids. It is also possible to use heavy card as a cutting board – the backs of old sketch pads are ideal.

T-squares

These are used in conjunction with a cutting board and are important for easily achieving perfect right-angled corners. Available in lightweight plastic from art shops, they are inexpensive and simple to use.

Patchworkers' rulers

These are also good for producing accurate angles. They come in all sorts of shapes and sizes, and are transparent, with measuring grids clearly marked in both metric and imperial units.

FABRICS

It is a good idea to have as wide a range of fabrics as possible. This need not entail vast expense. A good jumble sale will provide most fabrics at very little cost. Cotton sheets, linen table cloths (often with wonderful lace trims), silk shirts, velvet curtains and woollen blankets are the obvious ones, but there are often unexpected little treasures of special fabrics to be found at the humble jumble sales. These fabrics have the added benefit of being soft and used, with a quality of their own. Colour can be adjusted by bleaching and dyeing or painting.

Craft or pelmet Vilene

This most useful non-woven fabric is readily available from large stores.

Chiffon scarves

There really is no adequate alternative to the chiffon scarf, which is so thin as to be almost invisible on top of another surface, yet which can adjust colour and give durability to fragile surfaces.

Stitch'n'Tear

This is used as a backing during machining, when it supports and stabilizes fragile surfaces and difficult fabrics. It can be torn away after stitching.

THREADS

A bewildering and continually increasing array of machine threads is available, ranging from shiny to matt, thick to thin, and woolly to metallic. Buy good quality threads, and gradually build a range of colours and types.

There is also an exciting and inspiring range of hand-embroidery threads, and it is worth looking in remnant bins for balls of fine crochet cotton, or fancy knitting yarns and silky tapes.

NEEDLES

Needles come in many widths and lengths, each designed for a specific purpose, according to the characteristics of the threads they carry or the material to be stitched. Sharps are the most common, all-purpose, hand-sewing needles, but you will require additional types. Some of the most useful are listed below.

Beading needles

Designed for use with beads and sequins, these are exceptionally fine and long. They require a very fine thread to pass through the eye.

Crewel needles

These are sharp-pointed, with a long eye that enables the needle to carry more than one thread at the same time.

Chenille needles

These are short and pointed, with a large eye, and are ideal for working with chunky or coarse and textured threads.

Tapestry needles

Designed for needlepoint, the tapestry needle has a blunt end, intended for working on canvas or open-weaves, where you do not want the fabric threads to be pierced and split.

Bodkins

The bodkin is robust and blunt ended, with a very large eye, and can be used for threading ribbons, cords and the like through coarse fabric. Plastic versions can be bought in some craft shops and are often found in children's sewing kits.

Tea stirrers

Plastic stirrers of the type found in airport and railway station cafés, although flimsy, are very good for weaving ribbons or fabric strips through open mesh.

Sewing machine needles

A selection of machine needles designed for specific purposes is also an essential part of a good tool kit. Some useful varieties are listed here.

Topstitch needles

These have long, large eyes, enabling two or three threads to be passed through at the same time.

They also take metallic threads easily, as well as woolly types of machine thread.

Twin and triple needles

Designed to create two or three parallel lines of stitching, this type of needle can sometimes give the illusion of pin tucks. If worked through two layers of fabric, it provides fine channels through which threads can be pulled.

Vinyl needles

These have a narrow wedge-pointed tip for piercing vinyl, imitation leather and plastics.

FRAMES

On occasion, it is necessary to employ a frame to keep fabric taut, or to act as a support for threads. There are many types of frame on the market, each with its own particular strengths, but this list is limited to the sorts used for creating the surfaces in this book.

Tambour frames

These round frames, generally made of wood, are tightened by a screw and are excellent for keeping fabric very taut. The inner ring needs to be bound with a cotton tape, to avoid slippage and to protect the fabric. Tambour frames are ideal for both machine and hand embroidery.

Plastic spring frames

These have a metal inner ring and a plastic outer one. They are flatter than tambour frames, and ideal for machine work, when space between the needle and the machine bed is very limited. They do not hold the fabric as taut as tambour frames.

GENERAL SUPPLIES

An ironing surface

This is very useful, as an ironing board takes up a lot of space, and table-top boards can be unwieldy. An ironing surface is easy to make. Take a piece of plywood, or a couple of sheets of very heavy card, about 30 cm (12 in) square (or preferred size); wrap a layer of wadding around the square, and staple it at the back. On top, lay a piece of old ironing board cover; wrap it round and staple it firmly to the back of the board. Sew a piece of firmly woven cotton to the back to cover the staples.

Baking parchment

Available in rolls, from the baking section of supermarkets, this differs from greaseproof (wax) paper in that it is totally non-stick, and therefore has the same properties as the backing paper on commercial products such as Bondaweb. It is used to protect materials that must not come into direct contact with the iron. It is good practice to work with baking parchment as a matter of course when using the iron.

Marking pens and pencils

A good range of markers is a useful addition to the kit. Water- or air-soluble markers are useful if you require the original guidelines to disappear. Transfer pencils are ideal for tracing a design and ironing it to a surface, and tailors' chalk pencils make a line that can be brushed away.

PVA glue

This excellent multipurpose adhesive is white when applied, but dries to a plastic finish which is shiny, clear and durable. PVA must generally be used in small amounts, with only a very thin coating being applied. It

Wooden frames

Simple rectangular or square wooden frames, to which the fabric is attached with drawing pins or staples, are suitable for larger pieces of hand stitching. A simple frame can easily be made at home, or you can use an old picture frame instead. Small flat wooden frames, functioning in a similar way, are suitable for machine embroidery, when head space is limited beneath the needle.

Wire frames

These are particularly useful for winding networks of threads, ribbons, fibres and fabrics. The frame is very flat and is easy to use either for machining or for hand stitching and weaving. Available commercially in various sizes, they comprise two parts, which unslot for easy removal of work. A simple version is easily made from wire coat hangers, bent at right angles over a table edge. The ends are then fixed together with masking tape, for easy removal as necessary.

can be thinned with water, and can also be coloured with paints and powders, so in addition to its adhesive properties, it is also a good way of applying a durable coating to a surface.

Double-sided tape

This is useful as a quick and easy means of joining two surfaces together – fabrics can be peeled off it, but papers can not.

Wooden cocktail sticks

These have many uses, and are a basic essential. They are ideal for applying small amounts of PVA to stitched edges – for example, on boxes or book jackets – ensuring that threads are secure and wear-resistant.

They can be cut into different lengths for use as surface decoration or to be wrapped by machine or by hand.

They are an ideal tool for holding down threads and similar materials when free-machining. This safety measure ensures that fingers are not pierced, and if the machine needle should hit it, the stick merely splits, avoiding the possibility of a broken needle tip flying towards the face.

Protective masks

These should be part of your art kit. If you have one to hand, then you are more likely to follow safety procedures. It is possible to buy a mask that incorporates renewable filters for both dust and vapour. They are available at most Do-It-Yourself stores and also, increasingly, from art and craft suppliers.

Pliers

Snipe-nosed pliers are very useful, all-purpose pliers for making jewellery. Round-nosed pliers are good for coiling wire into spiral shapes.

ELECTRICAL GOODS

All electrical equipment should be tested periodically for electrical safety. Any electrical tool should always be used according to the manufacturer's instructions, and should be kept away from water.

Sewing machines

The increasingly sophisticated computer machines can be exciting, producing complex patterns and computer-aided designs. However, the samples in this book were created on a very old, basic machine, which has straight and zigzag stitches, and the facility to lower the feed dogs for free-machine embroidery.

Iron

Irons also vary in complexity, but the most suitable is the basic flat iron, without steam holes, on which the temperature control is accurate and simple.

Hair dryer

A hair dryer is very useful for drying painted materials.

Hot-air tool

This is used for embossing metal powders, and is available from stamping shops. It generates intense heat through a narrow nozzle that can be directed into small areas. Hot-air tools are particularly useful for raising puff paints, and distorting or distressing Tyveks, plastics and synthetic fabrics.

Soldering iron

Soldering irons of the sort used by model makers and craft workers are most useful for melting, burning and fusing certain materials. Those with a fine point offer the greatest potential. Use an upturned terracotta flower pot as a safe rest for the hot iron.

Stencil cutter

The stencil cutter is similar to a soldering iron, but has an angled tip, which can be more comfortable for the wrist.

Pyrography tool

Also known as a wood-burning iron, this is used for burning designs into wood or leather, and works on the same principle as the soldering iron. Pyrography tools are supplied complete with a plain-pointed tip and several interchangeable patterned ends, to give a variety of small designs. Depending upon how the tool is used, it is possible to obtain patterns or irregular textured areas on synthetic fabrics.

Chapter Two
Creating the Surfaces

This working section of the book deals with materials which, though perhaps not strictly plastics and films by industrial definition, we tend to think of as having plastic-like or film-like qualities.

▼ **Fig 1:**
Cut shapes before and after heating.

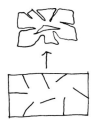

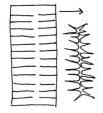

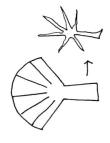

TYVEK FILM

Tyvek film is a very strong material that has many industrial applications because it is water-resistant and will not tear. It feels like a smooth fibrous film and looks like paper. With the application of heat, it shrinks, bubbles and distorts, giving enormous potential for creative uses.

It is available in different thicknesses, and can be coloured with a range of colouring media. It can also be fed through a printer, giving exciting possibilities for distorting text and image (check the manual for your particular printer if you intend using Tyvek in this way). Fabrics and threads can be added to the surface, and subsequent heating will create interesting raised textural surfaces for stitch. The film is heated beneath non-stick baking parchment, using an iron. It can also be heated with a hot-air tool (not a hairdryer), which gives a different effect. The following guidelines apply to all the stitched samples.

Requirements

- Tyvek film
- Paints in your chosen colours
- Brushes and water
- Ground fabrics and toning threads
- Baking parchment
- Iron and ironing surface
- Sewing kit
- Cocktail stick
- Sewing machine and thread

Colouring the film

The film can be coloured before or after heating.

The advantage of colouring beforehand is that when the film shrinks and distorts, wonderfully condensed areas of colour are created. The film can be coloured with inks, sprays paints and dyes, but bear in mind that the colouring media must be able to withstand the heat of an iron. Some colouring agents, particularly acrylic paints, can affect the rate of shrinkage, so it is a matter of experimenting to discover the differences.

Cutting the film

It is not generally possible to tear the film, so you will need to cut it either with scissors or with a fine-pointed soldering iron, which gives a softer edge to motifs. If using a soldering iron, place the painted film on a sheet of glass or an old ceramic tile before burning out the shape.

It is very important to bear in mind that the film can shrink to a fraction of its original size, so cut pieces much larger than you need them and experiment with the film to explore its properties. You must also be aware that cut lines will curl and creep away from each other (Fig 1).

Heating the film

Always place the film between two layers of baking parchment, and use the iron at wool/cotton setting. Move the iron over the whole surface, without pressing hard, to allow the film to rise and bubble as it shrinks. You will see through the paper. The shrinkage is visible through the baking parchment; if the iron is hot enough, this will happen very quickly, so watch carefully. Vary the iron temperatures and pressures for different effects – with experience you will learn how to achieve desired effects.

RAISED BUBBLES

This process requires some practice and, as with all melting processes, it is not possible to predict exactly what the results will be. It is a matter of experimenting until you get the feel of it. You will need to get to know your own particular iron, as each seems to have its own personality. You can use light, medium or heavyweight film – it is a matter of personal preference. Remember that the thinner the film, the faster it will react to the heat.

Preparing and heating

1   Paint the film, mixing and blending the colours on the film itself so that interesting secondary colours are made. Leave the film to dry.

2   Cut the film into squares, triangles or other shapes, measuring between 5 and 10 cm (2 and 4 in) each way. Do not make the shapes too small as they will shrink significantly.

3   Fold a piece of baking parchment in half and, for convex bubbles, place a piece of film, coloured side down, inside the fold. (For concave bubbling, place the film coloured side up in the sandwich.)

4   With the iron at wool/cotton setting, pass it over the surface, without pressing hard. Keep the iron moving slowly but steadily, so that the body of the iron passes over the whole piece. After three or four seconds, lift the iron and monitor what is happening – the film can shrink and bubble very quickly. Continue in this way until the surface has bubbled and distorted, always taking care not to press hard.

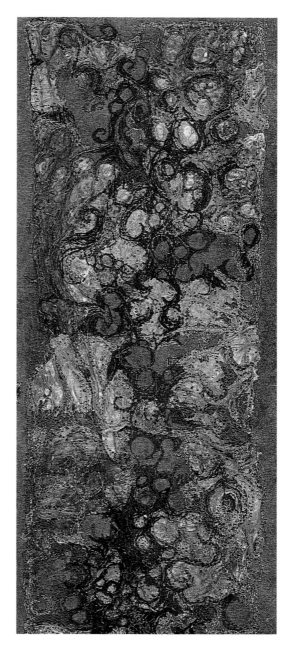

◄ **Fig 2:** Fragments of bubbled film sewn on to a painted ground. Machine stitching joined and unified the fragments.

5   When the film has bubbled sufficiently, remove it from the parchment sandwich and leave to cool – this will not take more than a minute. Turn the piece over to see the coloured bubbles raised upwards.

21

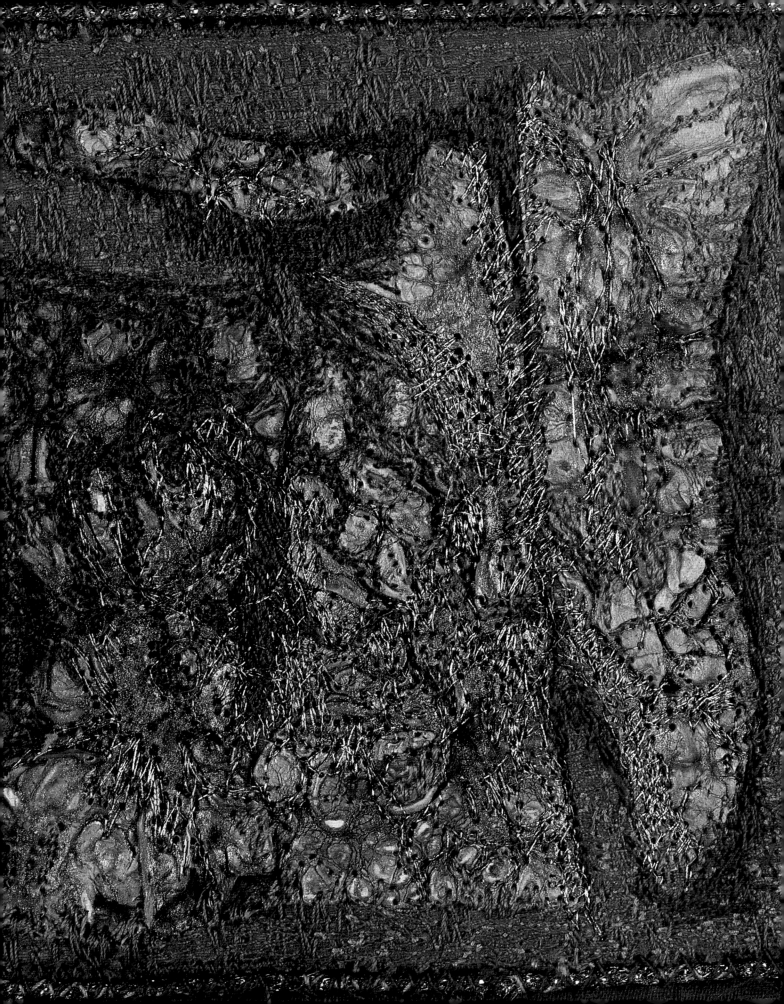

STITCHING

You will need to use your sewing machine in free-machining mode for this work, as it will be necessary to stitch in tight circular movements in order to blend the shapes together. Pin the bubbled shapes into place on the ground fabric, with just one pin in the centre of each patch. At this stage, they will look very unsubtle, but your stitching will overcome this. Leave some gaps between patches in some places, but allow them to touch at other points.

Using a thread chosen to match either the film or the ground fabric, free-machine the patches in position, using running stitch and sewing roughly around the edges of the patches. Hold the edges down with a wooden cocktail stick as you sew them. Stitch slowly, and go carefully over any very hard edges that may be difficult for the needle to pierce.

With all the patches secured, you must now consider how to blend them together, unifying them so that the work looks like one whole piece, instead of many fragments.

Look at the shapes made by the bubbles and 'draw' around them with your stitching for emphasis. Repeat these same movements and stitch across the ground fabric, linking one patch to the next. Echo the shapes and colours, changing the thread colour as necessary, to marry up colours and shapes.

Further ideas

You can apply cords and fabrics to the surface of the painted film before heating it. The film will shrink, but the additions will not (unless they are synthetic, in which case you have the opportunity to achieve further exciting effects), so the latter will distort and wrinkle, producing some very interesting results.

Before heating, you might consider some of the treatments listed below:

* Stitch the film randomly by machine, and consider zigzagging around the edges.
* Stitch by hand, using various thicknesses of thread and a range of stitches.
* Apply cords, chunky threads and braids, couching them down by hand or machine.
* Try adding sequins or other sparkly bits that could perhaps melt with heat, or sew on scraps of old thin lace, small oddments of fine fabrics, coloured fibres and foils.

Applied braids and cords

As with the basic method of applying random patches, it is important to echo the surface qualities with your stitching when applying your corded patches, following the rhythms made by the distortions.

Adding fabrics

Fabrics can be stitched over the surface of uncoloured film, using a range of stitching patterns to create different effects. It is best to use natural fabrics, such as cotton voile, muslins or fine silk – synthetic sheers may disintegrate. The fabrics should be very fine, so that they can ruche easily as the film distorts. Hand-dyed multi-shaded voiles are particularly effective.

* For linear ruching, lay the fabric on the film and sew parallel lines, regularly spaced. For a rounded bubbly ruching, sew around and around in figure-of-eight movements.
* Iron as already described, remembering that the film will shrink back from the heat. If you want convex fabric bubbles, iron fabric side down. For concave bubbles, iron fabric side up.

◄◄ **Fig 3:** Several patches of distorted film, applied to a ground fabric and machine-stitched freely to integrate.

▸ **Fig 4**: Three
different patches
were made, using
leather cords,
machine cords and
braid, plus random
machine-stitching.
The distorted
patches were then
pinned to a
background of
metallic fabric and
Vilene and stitched
with toning
threads, to
emphasize the
surface distortions.

▸▴ ▸ ▸▸**Figs 5, 6
and 7**: Linear,
concave and convex
bubble ruching.

24

FILIGREE AND LACEWORK

Taking things a stage further than simple heating and bubbling, it is possible to achieve some very exciting filigree or lacelike effects. Once more, it is a question of practising to acquire a familiarity with the medium – the more you experiment, the more control you will ultimately have over the process.

Bubble two pieces of coloured film as already described – try one with the coloured side up and the other with the coloured side down, so that you discover the differences. When the pieces have cooled, place them bubble side up within the parchment sandwich, and gently rest the iron on them, so that the tops of the bubbles are melted away. Depending on the heat of your iron, this will take a few seconds. Do not press hard or you will flatten the pieces. Keep going until you are satisfied with the amount of holes produced.

The size and distribution of holes will clearly depend upon the nature of the bubbles you produced in the first place. Often the bigger the piece of film used, the larger the bubbles, but you will need to discover what works best for you – try different sizes and weights of film.

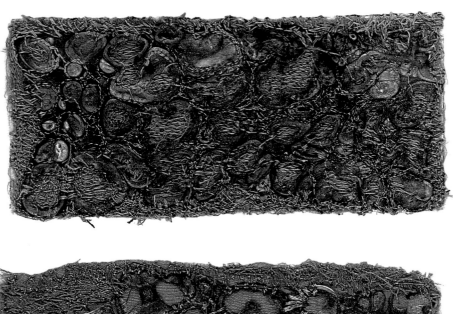

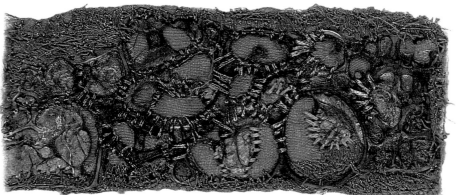

◀ **Fig 9**: This piece was initially ironed colour-side up, so the ridges were standing proud. The piece was then placed on a ground of cotton voile on top of heavyweight Vilene. Subsequent stitching was by machine around the edges, and by hand, with heavy thread over the ridges.

▼◀ **Fig 8**: In this sample, the bubbles have been thoroughly melted away, by resting the iron on the surface for a longer time, and by applying slightly more pressure, so that the piece is somewhat flatter, and generally more disintegrated. It has been freely stiched in flowing lines that echo the shapes, on to a firm ground. The gold colour of the film has been taken into the blue ground fabric, and blue thread has been used to take the colour of the fabric into the stitched areas of film, ensuring that the two surfaces blend harmoniously.

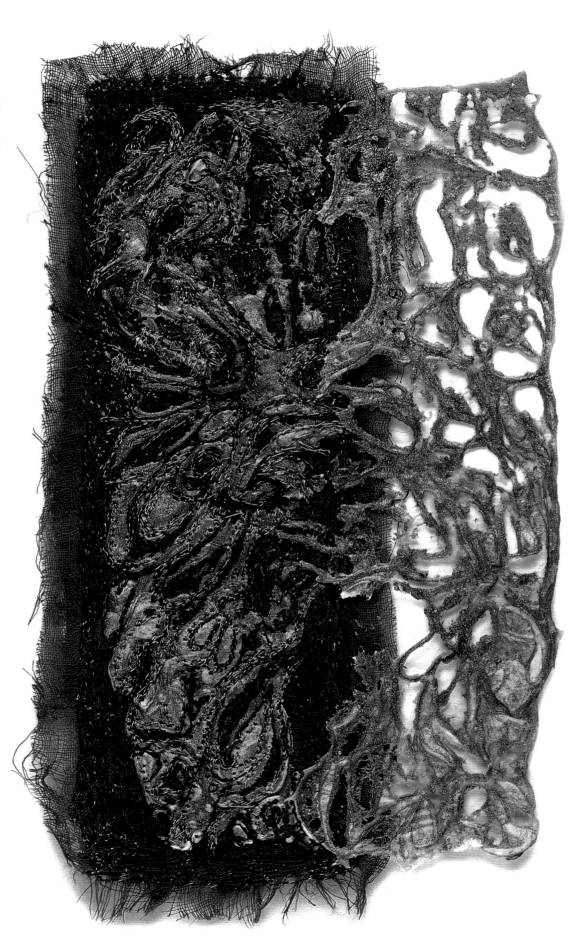

▶ **Fig 10:** Partially stitched sample. Gold-painted Tyvek film has bubbled then been ironed to near disintegration. It was placed on blue voile and Vilene, then stitched in gold and blue threads to merge with the background.

DISTORTING AN IMAGE

A picture was scanned into a computer and printed on Tyvek. The whole sheet was carefully ironed in the usual manner, with very frequent monitoring to check that the image had not shrunk too much.

The distorted piece was then placed on black firm cotton and the picture details redrawn in straight stitch, using threads of an appropriate colour, to redefine shapes and objects. The outer edges were similarly extended into the black fabric, maintaining the now irregular outside shape.

Further ideas

- Scan your own photographs of people and places, print them on an A4 sheet and distort – but check the printer manual first to ensure that it can accommodate Tyvek sheet.
- Type the text and print it out, or write on film with a felt pen and then warp the lettering.

Note that it would be inadvisable to use a photocopier as the heat might cause problems.

◄ **Fig 11:** This piece was based on a picture of a painting by Georges Braques, which was scanned into a computer and printed on a sheet of medium-weight Tyvek.

STRIPS AND STRIPES

Note that in addition to the usual materials you will require cords or narrow braids.

Preparing strips

1 Cut Tyvek film into several strips of varying widths and lengths. The edges may either be straight or wavy. Shrink the strips within a baking parchment sandwich; if you shrink them one at a time, you will have a little more control over the process.

2 For flat strips, use a medium pressure, and move the iron continuously, checking regularly to monitor the shrinkage. After three or four seconds, turn the parcel over and iron the other side – this is not always necessary, but it helps to keep the strip flat.

3 For a more rounded, cordlike effect, use strips 1 cm (1/2 in) in width, and iron with a light pressure and the coloured side down, within the parchment paper sandwich.

You now have all the components for creating an interesting surface of strips.

▼ **Fig 12:** Strips and stripes.

Stitching

Select your background fabric with care, making sure that it is sympathetic to the quality of your strips, in terms of weight and colour. Here, plain blue cotton voile was placed on a piece of Vilene, and stitched freely, with a matching top thread and a gold thread in the bobbin. The top tension was tightened so that dots of gold thread appeared from beneath. These small specks of gold helped the gold strips to marry up with the ground fabric. The strips were then sewn on by hand, using simple stitching and both matching and contrasting threads.

After you have applied each strip, consider how to echo its linear nature, before applying the next. Here, ridges of fabric were pinched up to stand proud of the surface. They were then emphasized by being oversewn with a contrasting thread. Occasionally, a machine-made gold cord was applied, creating stripes on a smaller scale.

Further ideas

- Hand wrap the strips with thread or fine fabric before you heat them.
- Change the colour and scale of threads used to apply the strips. Make a feature of the stitches and use thread of a contrasting colour.
- Change the direction of the strips, and the spaces between them.

TYVEK FABRIC

Tyvek is also available in a soft fabric-like version. Its fabric-like qualities make it easy to manipulate and to hand stitch, and it can be also be free-machined like a fabric. It can easily be knotted or woven, and strips can readily be used for wrapping techniques. Used with wire, it offers exciting possibilities for three-dimensional work.

Requirements

The same equipment is required as for Tyvek film. In addition, you may need a hot-air tool, a few plastic-headed pins, and a heating surface that is sufficiently soft to take pins, such as a pile of newspapers or an ironing board.

Heating methods
Iron

Follow the same procedures as for Tyvek film, ironing without pressure and monitoring carefully.

Hot-air tool

Place the stitched piece, coloured side up, on a soft, heat-resistant surface, such as a covered ironing board, and hold it down with one pin through the centre. It is advisable to use a plastic-headed pin rather than a metal-headed one, as the former will not retain so much heat.

Holding the hot air tool about 15 cm (6 in) above the fabric, gradually work your way around the outer sides of the piece, moving the tool slowly and evenly. The edges will curl up and over towards the centre of the piece. Do not panic! Continue to move the tool slowly and evenly around until the edges have curled right in. Turn the heat off. Remove the pin, straighten out the edges and turn the piece over so that the partly shrunken work is face down. Secure with the pin as before, and apply the hot air again, working quickly around the edges and finally into the centre, before removing the pin and straightening the piece.

If you want the work to have a disintegrated look, it is possible to pull the fabric gently at the fully heated stage, stretching holes into the piece, or you might even tear it apart.

PLEATS AND TUCKS

1 Colour a piece of Tyvek fabric about 20 cm (8 in) square, using at least two colours, and paint some ordinary fabric in the same colours, so that you have a compatible ground fabric.

2 Pinch a pleat along the length of the Tyvek and stitch close to the fold line, using either free machining or automatic stitching. Repeat this at close intervals until you have a series of pintucks.

3 Cut the pin-tucked piece into patches, varying the angles of cut.

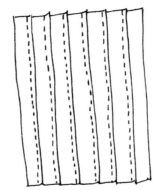 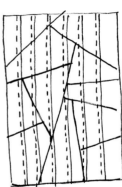

◀◀ **Fig 13:** Stitched pintucks.
◀ **Fig 14:** Cutting the stitched piece.

> **HAZARD ALERT!**
> The more you heat it, the more fluid the material becomes, and the more it retains heat. Take care when straightening out the edges

4 Stitch the patches together, so that the pin-tucked lines change direction at the joins. Either butt the edges or slightly overlap them.

5 You will end up with an irregularly shaped patchwork. Shrink and distort this, using either the iron or the hot air tool, as described above.

6 Work similar pintucking on the ground fabric, then cut this up and reassemble it in the same way.

7 Pin the Tyvek fabric piece to the ground fabric, and free-machine into the grooves, extending the stitching into the ground fabric to merge the two together.

Change the colour of the thread, according to the colour of the distorted piece, and stitch so as to maximize the joins and differences in colour.

LAYERS AND PATCHES

Tyvek fabric can be patched, layered and stitched in a similar way to woven fabrics, and the subsequent shrinking gives exciting and often unexpected results.

1 Take two or three pieces of Tyvek fabric, each a different colour and each measuring about 10 x 6 cm (4 x 2¹/² in). Cut simple shapes from one piece and place them upon another, stitching around the edges to join. Use any stitch you like, as long as it encloses the edges.

2 Continue in this way until you have a pleasing patch. Further embellish the surface with other stitches, such as French knots, bullions, and so on.

3 Finally, stitch around the outside edge of the entire patch to enclose it.

4 Heat and shrink the piece as previously described. The hot-air tool is generally more effective, giving a more distorted and irregular finish. However, if you are seeking a flatter, more controlled effect, use an iron.

Further ideas

- Try a variety of hand stitches – each will give a different result.
- Add cords and beads or sequins, first making sure that they can withstand heat.
- Cut slashes in the upper patches, so that the lower colour is revealed as they shrink and open up.

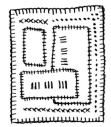

◀◀ Fig 15: Pleats and tucks.

▼ Fig 16: A selection of hand-stitched patches.

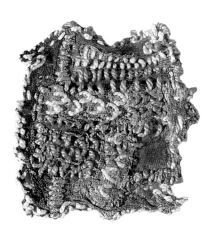

▶ **Fig 17:** Three Tyvek fabric patches, sewn to a toning ground fabric. Each patch was made by sewing a blue piece on to an orange piece, then applying chunky threads to the surface, followed by random stitching.

▶▶ **Fig 18:** Machined patches, shrunk, then layered upon each other.

▼ **Fig 19:** Wired pieces were heated individually until the fabric had nearly disintegrated, and then layered.

▶ ▼ **Fig 20:** Suggested positions for wires.

MACHINED PATCHES

Machine stitching creates a very different effect to hand stitching. It is easy to couch chunky threads and cords in place with zigzag stitch. Patches can be planned and fairly regular, or completely random and haphazard – both have their attractions.

Adding wires

Couch fine wires to the Tyvek with zigzag stitch. Remember that as the work shrinks, so the wires will creep closer together. Use snipe- or round-nosed pliers to bend the ends into shape. Try various placings of the wire to discover the many possibilities for forming different shapes before or after heating. You might make several wired pieces and layer them.

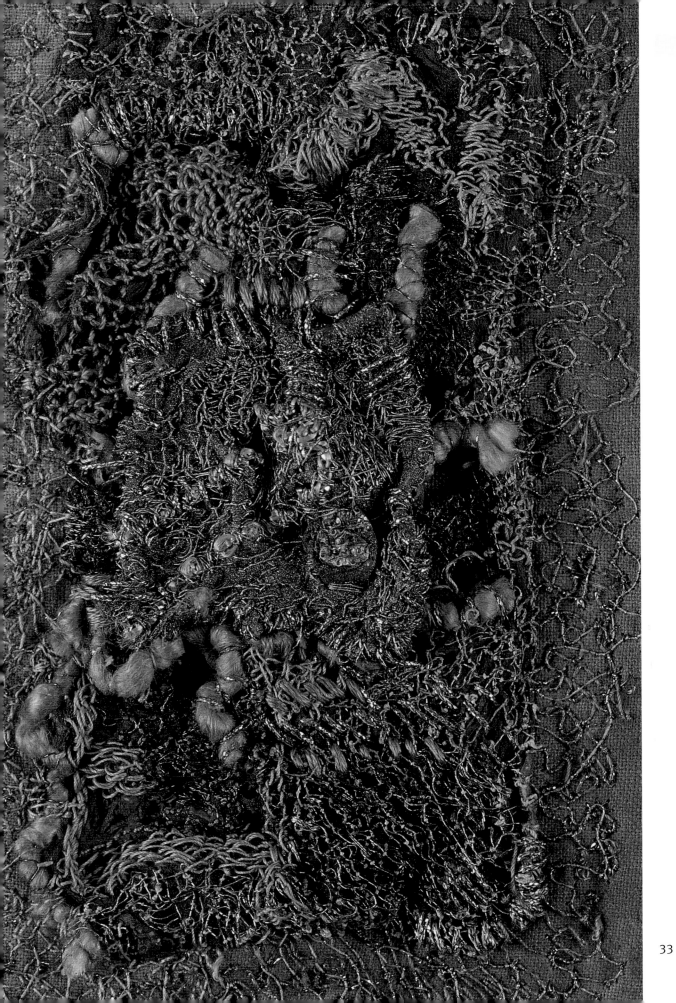

▾ **Fig 21:** A
skeleton design.

▸▸ **Fig 22:**
Disintegrated layers,
machine stitched on
to a fabric ground.

DISINTEGRATED LAYERS

You will need a hot air tool for this technique, as an iron will give different results to those illustrated.

1 Take three or four pieces of Tyvek fabric, each of a different colour and each measuring about 15 x 12 cm (6 x 4³/₄ in) and lay them, with the coloured side up, on top of each other. Tack (baste) through all layers to hold them together.

2 Turn the pile over and draw a simple design on the white underside of the pile.

3 With the coloured side down, and the design uppermost, machine several times over the

lines until you have very firm and dense lines of stitching. Remember that the colour in the bobbin is the colour that will show on the front of your work.

Heating

4 With the coloured side uppermost, pin the piece to a soft ironing surface, placing the pins at approximately 2 cm (³/₄ in) intervals all around the edges, so that the layered fabric is firmly held in place.

5 Apply the hot air, working slowly and evenly across the piece. It will be unable to shrink because of the pins holding it in place. Consequently, the layers will melt in turn, each revealing the colour of the layer beneath. Move quickly, or raise the tool away when you get to the required layer. Watch carefully, as the melting takes place quickly.

6 Stitch the piece to a ground fabric of a sympathetic colour. You can redefine areas of colour and adjust designs with your stitching, redrawing what you have melted away, to achieve a crisp line of a different texture.

Further ideas

• Pin the layered fabric out as before, but allow all the layers to be melted away, so that you end up with a stitched skeleton design.

• To achieve a distorted effect, omit the pins around the edges, and allow the piece to shrink and distort freely. The piece will be smaller and irregular in shape, and the design lines will be thicker and chunkier in nature. Hand stitch over some of the design before shrinking the fabric, to create robust design lines and textured areas of stitch.

WRAPPING TECHNIQUES

Creating unusual beads from Tyvek fabric is simple. You need a long wooden stick, such as a kebab-type barbecue stick, a hot-air tool for antiqued beads, and a soldering iron for incised beads.

MAKING SCULPTURAL BEADS

1   Cut two strips of painted Tyvek fabric, each of a different colour and each about 3 cm (1¼ in) wide and 25 cm (10 in) long, and place one on top of another, white sides up. It doesn't matter if the measurements are not exact.

2   Place a long wooden stick on the white side and wrap towards you – uneven edges and misshapes will not matter. Continue rolling the stick along the length of the strip. Hold the end of the fabric-covered stick with your thumb and begin wrapping it with thread.

3   Start the continuous wrapping by leaving a long thread so that the eventual tying off is easy. Have some metallic thread ready. This must be a type that will stand the heat. Bind the stick tightly, on the spot, then move further along with the same thread and repeat the process, so that you have three or four areas of solid wrapping. Now wrap randomly along the bead and back before tying off with a secure double knot.

4   Holding the far end of the stick to ensure safety, position the hot-air tool with the nozzle about 10 cm (4 in) away from the wrapping, and direct the hot air at the bead, aiming first at the ends, to seal them, and then along the wrapped length, turning the stick, so that the heat is evenly distributed.

The thread acts as a resist, so the heat does not penetrate the layers. Between the wrapped areas, the coloured layers are melted, revealing the colours beneath. The more you heat, the deeper the erosion, and the more sculptural the bead.

5   While it is still warm, roll the bead in the hands before removing it from the stick. Take care – metal threads may retain heat

Further ideas

• Increase the number of colours in the wrapped strips, using more layers and shorter lengths.

• Wrap once and bind with a coloured sparkly thread, and then wrap again and bind thoroughly before heating – your layers will reveal further glimpses of thread.

• Change the widths, lengths and shapes of the strips to vary the shapes of your beads.

▶▶**Figs 25 (overleaf):** Sculptural beads by Silvia Hedley.

▶**Fig 23:** Step 2 wrapping for sculptural beads.

▶**Fig 24:** Step 3 Tying.

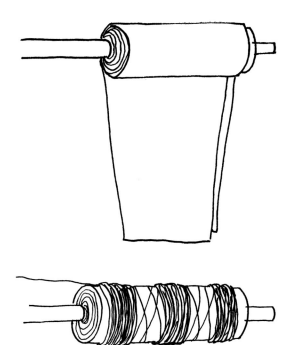

INCISED BEADS

1. Prepare a heated fine-tipped soldering iron.
2. Cut two strips of coloured Tyvek fabric, place one on the other and wrap on a stick, as described for sculptural beads (see page 36).
3. Holding the (unwrapped) end of the strip firmly in place with your thumb, press the soldering iron across the join, so that it immediately melts through a couple of layers, sealing them together.
4. Continue in this way, changing the direction of the soldering iron to create patterns. Insert the tip to produce incised holes and dots.
5. Slide the soldering iron along the surface of the stick, pushing it into the ends of the bead and turning it evenly, so as to seal and solidify the ends.
6. Finish by removing the bead from the stick.

Further ideas
- Plan the incised patterns – many designs can be made from simple straight lines.
- Wrap the stick first with a strip 4 cm (1½ in) wide and then a second coloured wrapping 2 cm (5/8 in) wide, to create beads with a 'step'. Consider different contours and colours.
- Draw into the bead with the tip of the soldering iron. Do not press too hard, or the iron will become difficult to manoeuvre.

More wrapping suggestions
- Wrap, as if using ordinary fabric, along the length of cocktail sticks, lollipop sticks, spills and twigs, using coloured strips about 1 cm (½ in) wide. Bind and tie the strips with coloured threads, then wrap again and bind before heating.
- Assemble a bundle of heated sticks, and wrap the bundle before heating yet again.
- Use sticks to create three-dimensional structures, binding and tying at the intersections.
- Sew pieces into the open areas of open structures and heat these to distress them.
- Wrap a small block of thin wood in a larger piece of coloured Tyvek fabric, as if wrapping a parcel, and tie securely with a decorative thread in both directions. Repeat, using a second colour and a metallic thread tie, before heating to reveal layers and thread beneath.

▸▸**Fig 29:**
5 wrapped parcels.

▸ **Fig 27:**
Tied sticks.

▸ **Fig 28:**
Wrapped sticks in bundles.

Fig 30 (overleaf):
Incised beads.

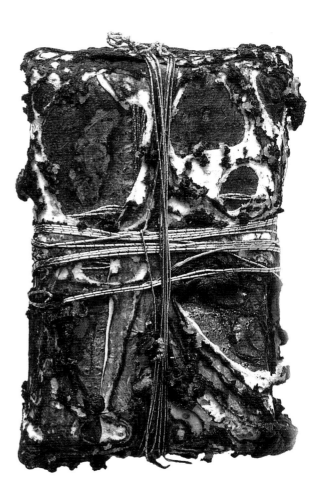

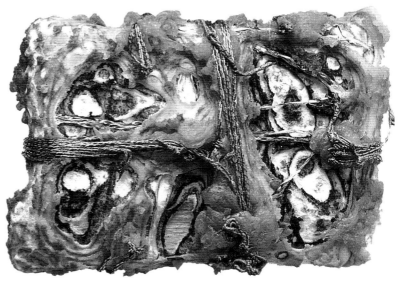

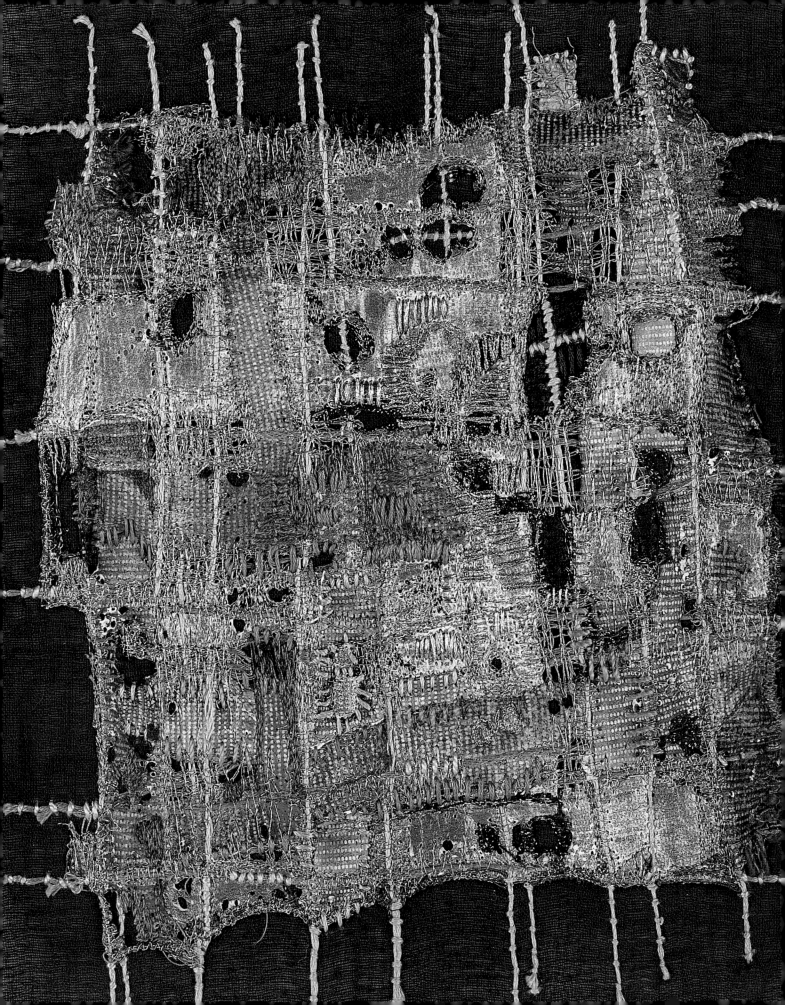

WOVEN AND STITCHED STRIPS

Requirements

- A frame (suitable for machine stitching)
- Thread to make a grid
- Painted Tyvek strips
- Machine threads
- Sewing machine

1   Knot the thread to the frame, and wrap randomly, first vertically and then horizontally, to create a gridlike structure for weaving.

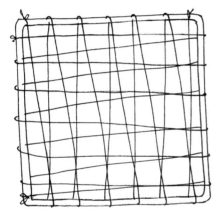

2   Weave Tyvek fabric strips of varying widths randomly in and out in both directions. Some threads will still be visible on the surface.

3   Keeping the structure in the frame, machine stitch randomly in both directions over the surface of the woven piece and all around the edge. Do not cut the work from the frame.

4   Using the hot-air tool, direct the heat from about 12 cm (4³/₄ in) above, moving steadily over the entire area. The woven strips will shrink and distort to reveal the threads, and holes will appear in places.

5   Cut the woven piece out from the edges of the frame. It can then be applied to a ground fabric with further machine and hand stitching, or used for a section in three-dimensional work or any other way you wish.

Alternative finish

After you have cut the weaving from the frame, secure it – colour-side up – to a suitable board with a central pin, and heat to it to shrink and distort it freely. Turn the piece over and repeat the process. You will now have a very irregular and distorted sample of weaving, with wiggly lines of fabric and thread, to use as a basis for further stitchery.

◄ **Fig 31:**
A woven and stitched piece, machine stitched on to fabric.

▼ **Fig 32:**
Woven sample heated off frame.

KNOTTED TEXTURES

1 Colour Tyvek fabric on both sides, and cut into strips of 3 cm (1¼ in) wide. Knot them together to make longer lengths if necessary.

2 Tie knots along the length at intervals of between 3 and 5 cm (1¼ and 2 in). You can tie one knot on top of another to make large chunky knots.

3 Pin each length to a suitable board, placing a single pin in the centre of the strip, and apply heat to distort and shrink the strip.

You will produce knobbly gnarled-looking strips which are suitable for couching to fabrics, or perhaps for use in wrapping or other creative applications.

Further ideas

- Vary the gaps between the knots, and the sizes of the knots themselves. Thread heat-resistant beads along the strips before tying knots.

- When knotting the strips, incorporate interesting threads or fine fabric, laying them along the strips so that that they are tied in with the knots.

▶ **Fig 36:** Knotted strips couched on to a ruched ground fabric.

POLYTHENE AND PLIABLE PLASTICS

Polythene carrier bags are easily available from supermarkets and other stores, yielding a free supply of coloured polythene sheets which, with a gentle heat, can be fused together. This results in exciting possibilities for creating surfaces ranging from the very fragile to the very robust, depending on the number of layers fused together.

Start a collection of bags, gathering as many colours as possible and saving all the lettering and logos that you find – you may well want to use text in your work. You will find that the bags come in different thicknesses, ranging from fairly heavy ones to very thin 'one-trip' bags, all of which are useful. The very flimsy bags, which are almost transparent, can be used to overlay and subdue the brighter ones, creating interesting tonal effects.

The following guidelines apply to all of the stitched samples.

Requirements
- A pair of small sharp scissors
- Basic sewing kit
- A selection of polythene carrier bags
- An iron and ironing surface
- Non-stick baking parchment
- Colouring materials, if needed – these are optional

Cutting the polythene

For straight lines, use either sharp scissors or a craft knife, board and safety ruler. You can tear a bag if you make a nick in it first. This can produce a frilly, irregular edge and often stretches the colour to a paler shade, which is useful for random effects and soft lines.

Colouring

It is much easier to work with the colours that you have collected – part of the character of this work is its range of strong colours. However, if you want colours or effects that are not available, then try various colouring agents. It is sometimes difficult to make colour adhere to the polythene, and the paint must be thick. Some acrylics work fairly well when used straight from the container without adding water. Make small samples to see what works best.

Heating

It is important not to have the iron too hot. A gentle heat is needed, with the iron set at silk/wool, so that the layers fuse without melting and disintegrating. The hotter the iron, the less control you will have, and the greater the likelihood that the polythene will be destroyed.

Remember! Always put the pieces between two sheets of baking parchment, and never allow polythene to come into contact with the iron.

Allow the work to cool for a few seconds before you peel the paper away slowly, as the polythene may stretch if still too warm.

It is always possible to add more layers after the initial fusing – either to strengthen the back of the piece, or to add to the design at the front.

RANDOM PATCHING AND PIECING

1   Lay a sheet of non-stick baking parchment on a soft ironing surface, then over this lay two pieces of polythene, about 15 cm (6 in) square, one on top of the other. These pieces will act as a base, so their colour doesn't matter, as they will not be seen.

2   Now cut or rip areas of polythene of several colours and lay them on top of the base. Gradually build up another two layers, of various colours, sizes and shapes, placing the pieces randomly overlapping each other.

3   Place another piece of baking parchment over the entire surface of the layers.

4   With the iron set at silk/wool, heat the parcel, pressing firmly and moving the iron evenly over the surface. The aim is to warm the polythene sufficiently to fuse the layers, but without causing them to melt and disintegrate.

5   Leave the parcel to cool for about 30 seconds, then gradually peel back the parchment. If the layers have not fused, repeat the procedure, with a slightly higher temperature. The layers should be well fused together, to produce a multi-coloured sheet of flexible but strong polythene that is both smooth and robust.

If you wish to add more shapes or colours to the sheet, simply lay them on top and repeat the procedure.

If you feel that the piece ought to be thicker, you can turn it over, lay another complete layer on the back, and heat as before.

Using the sheet

- Machine or hand stitch into it, emphasizing the shapes and colours.
- Stitch fabrics and threads to the surface for further interest.
- Cut out pieces to use for appliqué, or for beads and surface additions

◀◀ **Fig 34:** A piece partially worked to show before and after stitching.

▼ **Fig 35:** These irregular bottle-like shapes have been hand stitched to emphasize the outlines.

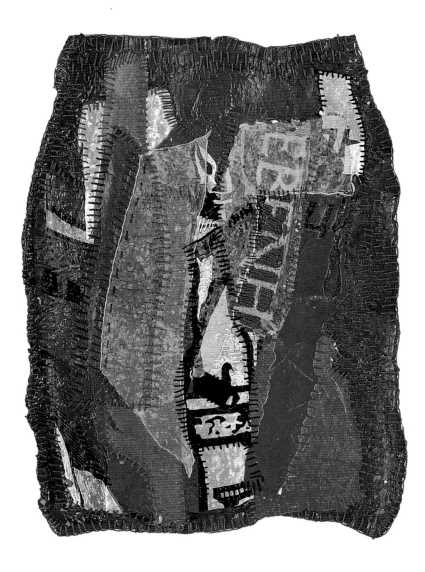

CUT DESIGNS AND MOSAICS

The cream-based tile on this sample was inspired by designs from an ancient tiled floor. The design demanded rich colours that were uneven and merged into one another. To achieve this, a polythene bag was turned inside out and painted with acrylic paints (Liquitex). The tile and the background were made separately and fused afterwards. Patterns from another source could well have been interpreted in the vibrant plain bold colours of ready-coloured carrier bags.

▼ Fig.36: Tile on mosaic background.

The tile

1 On a sheet of baking parchment, place a layer of polythene of the required size of the tile, bearing in mind that the polythene may shrink slightly upon heating.

2 Lay a second sheet on top; this will be the actual ground colour of your tile.

3 Cut out your design from the other colours you have chosen, and carefully position the shapes on the tile.

4 Lay a second sheet of baking parchment over the top, and iron gently over the entire surface, pressing firmly.

   If there are many small pieces to be fused, there is often a tendency for them to shift as you lay the top parchment in place. A way round this is to fuse the design in instalments, ironing for just for a second or so, then laying on the next set of cut pieces and repeating until all the design is down securely. At this stage, iron more firmly, so that the entire piece is fused well together. It is possible to fuse a very small area with just the tip of the iron.

5 Leave the fused piece to cool within the parchment sandwich, before peeling back carefully.

6 Turn the tile over and repeat.

If you plan to use the tile as it is, without fusing it to a background, you may like it to be thicker. Perhaps, for example, you might intend to apply intensive stitchery, in which case you can add another layer or two to the back and fuse as before.

The mosaic ground

1 Lay down a base of parchment covered with polythene.

2 Cut squares and rectangles at random, using all the colours found in the tile patterning, but not the background colour of the tile itself.

3 Place these shapes on your base in no particular order, overlapping them slightly.

4 Place parchment on top, and iron the sandwich for just a couple of seconds to lightly fuse.

5 Peel back the parchment, then place the tile on the mosaic.

6 Cover with parchment, and iron firmly, paying particular attention to areas where the edges of the tile and the mosaic border join.

7 Turn the piece over and iron firmly again, before peeling back .

Further ideas

• Using small squares of colour, plan a more regular design based, for example, on classic Roman mosaics.

• Set up your own simple still life of flowers and perhaps fruit; cut shapes directly from the polythene and place them on a background colour.

• Cut out elements, based on folk art designs, and create a pictorial piece.

• Use letters and numbers to make a message and create text within a piece.

To stitch or not?

The charm of many of these fused patterns lies in the softened edges of the design and the varying surface qualities caused by the fusing. Often, they are most effectively enhanced with minimal stitching, which merely emphasizes line and colour. Having said that, however, it could easily happen that a robust sample of patching and piecing might cry out for rugged machine- or hand- stitching, so the general rule is to let the nature of the piece dictate the type of stitching.

STITCHING FIRST

Interesting line, pattern, motif and texture can be achieved by stitching the polythene before the heating process. Subsequent heating, if prolonged, results in much of the polythene being melted away, leaving the lines of stitching intact. This produces a pattern of eroded gaps and holes in a piece which is most effective when fused to a sheet of a contrasting colour. Motifs and patterns made in this way have a slight distortion, which attractively softens the shapes and adds to the aged effect. The samples shown are not complete in themselves. They will need further stitching and blending into a ground material.

Requirements

- Sewing machine and threads
- Polythene in two contrasting colours
- Parchment and iron
- Marker (if you intend drawing a specific motif)

Motif or pattern

Note that all stitching is worked through two layers of polythene.

1 Draw your pattern or motif on a piece of polythene and place it on a second piece, pinning the layers together at the outside for ease of stitching.

2 Stitch round your design three times to produce a heavy line.

3 Cut the shape out, either fairly close to the lines or leaving a rectangle, square or other shape around it. Place this in a baking parchment sandwich.

4 Do not press too heavily to begin with, so that the piece can shrink at the edges. When this is done, press more firmly, and iron until the piece starts to disintegrate and holes appear. Carry on until you have the required degree of distress.

5 While the piece is still warm, it can be gently pulled to distress it further, if needed.

6 Cut a piece of polythene of a contrasting colour, a bit bigger than the stitched piece, and lay one on the other. Check both sides of the stitched piece – you may prefer one side to the other.

7 Place the piece in a parchment sandwich and iron both sides, pressing firmly. Cool and remove. If you feel that the piece needs either to be thicker or reshaped at the edges, you can add more layers to the back and fuse as before.

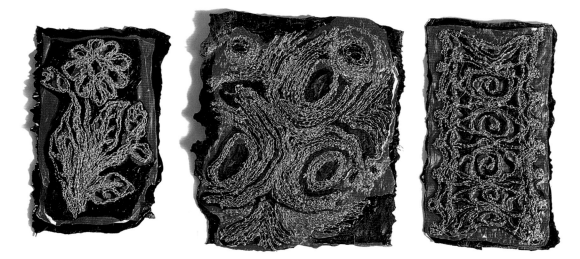

▶ **Fig 37** (3 pieces): Floral motif and patterns .

NETS AND WEBS

Eye-catching nets and webs are easily created by heating finely cut strips of polythene, placed at random. The thinner the strips, the finer the web will be. The advantage of creating nets by this method lies in the sheer randomness of the results. The strips of polythene will vary in width, and the heating process further erodes and softens the edges. The resulting designs are reminiscent of jagged winter undergrowth and bare branches against a winter sky.

1. Roll a piece of polythene roughly into a tube, or scrunch it up in your hand.

2. Cut across the roll or bunch of polythene, so that a long strip, between 2 and 3 mm ($1/12$ and $1/8$ in) wide falls at random on to a piece of baking parchment.

3. Continue in this way, letting the cut pieces fall at will and allowing them to crisscross haphazardly. Continue until you have a fairly even covering that fills the desired area.

4. Cover with baking parchment and iron for just a few seconds, to fuse. Cool and remove.

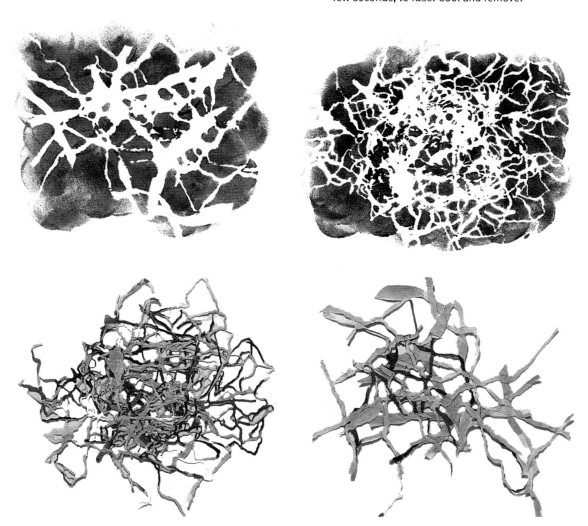

◀ **Fig 38:** Thick and thin nets with stencil prints.

Further ideas

- Cut a scant layer of strips of one colour, followed by different colours for subsequent layers.
- Vary the widths of the cut strips, so that the net has thick and thin filaments.
- Lay strands of thread and other fibres among the strips before fusing.
- Try placing small scraps of fabric with a very open weave, such as scrim, in between the layers.
- Place cut or torn coloured shapes in places, producing some solid areas on the net.

Using the basic net as a stencil

If you stencil through the net on to fabric, you will have a patterned ground that is compatible with the net itself, to use for further stitching. Lay the net on fabric or paper, and hold down firmly with one hand. Using a stencil brush or dry sponge, dab vertically, making sure that the net does not move. Over-print with a second colour if desired, slightly offsetting it for a 'ghosting' effect.

▼ Fig 39:
A raised net stitched onto a printed ground.

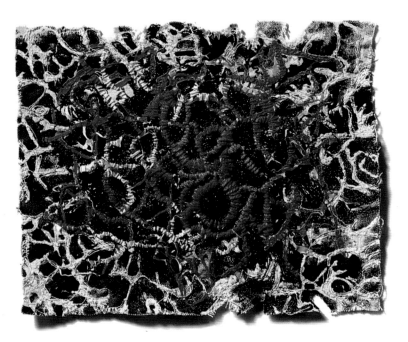

STITCHING FOR A RAISED NET

Requirements

- A coloured net
- Printed (through the net) ground fabric
- A piece of polythene to match the printed colour (black in this case)
- Sewing machine
- Machine threads to match net
- Hand-stitching threads in various weights

1. Cut the polythene to a shape just smaller than the net, and sew it to the printed fabric. Randomly stitch all over in a matching thread to create texture.
2. Using free-machining, first outline and then fill in the shapes that are printed. Use Stitch'n'Tear or a similar product beneath the work if necessary. Be sure to blend the edges of the polythene patch and the printed ground fabric with stitching, so that there are no harsh edges.
3. Lay the net on top of the patch and stitch along some of the lines in a matching thread. It is not necessary to stitch thoroughly or on every single line. The purpose is to hold the net into place for further hand stitching – too much machining will flatten it.
4. Decide upon a main area of interest or focal point, and hand stitch over this area with a thick chunky thread, couching the lines fairly densely, so that they stand out as ridges. As you work towards the outside of the net, select thinner threads and make the stitching less dense, so that the effect is lighter and flatter than in the main area. You may wish to leave some parts of the net standing away from the background.

WINDOWS AND INSERTS

It is possible to create framed single- or multi-windowed pieces. The windows can be of any shape you wish, offering endless possibilities for varied arrangements. You could simply leave a window empty, or fill it with something else, such as fine scrim, open vegetable nets, sequin waste and so on. Another option is to fill the window partially by suspending something within the space.

A basic window

Cut two or three squares or rectangles of strong polythene to the required size. Remove the central areas with scissors, to produce windows. Lay the windows on top of each other on a piece of baking parchment. Add any further patterns or decoration to the top layer.

Place a second piece of baking parchment over the top and iron firmly, to fuse. Remove the window from the parchment.

For a window with irregular edges, place extra patches of polythene around the borders, so that they overlap the sides, and then fuse.

INSERTING A NET

Requirements

- A window with a patched border
- Narrow strips of polythene
- A net in a toning colour, larger than the hole to be covered
- Hand-sewing kit
- Hand-stitching threads
- Iron and baking parchment

1 Lay the window on the parchment, right side down, and place the net on top. Lay the strips of polythene over the outer parts of the net, on the borders of the window, so that the edges are totally covered. It does not matter if the strips lie slightly over the window borders at each side, as this will add to the softness of the edges, and give a random feel to the piece. Cover and fuse the new layers to the others.

2 Using hand threads and simple outline stitching, decorate the border patches. Stitches may tone or contrast, depending on your preference. Oversew the outside edges.

3 Take a threaded needle and, starting from the back of the piece with a strong knot, weave a thread from one side of the window to the other. At the side, secure the thread with a double stitch at the back of the work, sliding the needle in between the layers so that the securing stitches are not seen on the right side of the work.

4 Continue in this way, working one woven thread at a time and securing it off, until you have enough crisscrossing threads to give the effect you require. Try to keep the tension even, so that the piece does not have slack or loopy threads. It may well distort slightly – this all adds to the overall qualities of the piece.

Further ideas

- Weave with paper, strips of torn fabric or plastic ribbons and gift tapes.
  Thread beads or found objects on to the needle and thread as you weave, making the objects an integral part of the woven web.
  Patch a contrasting colour or shape to the back of the net, as you sew and weave.

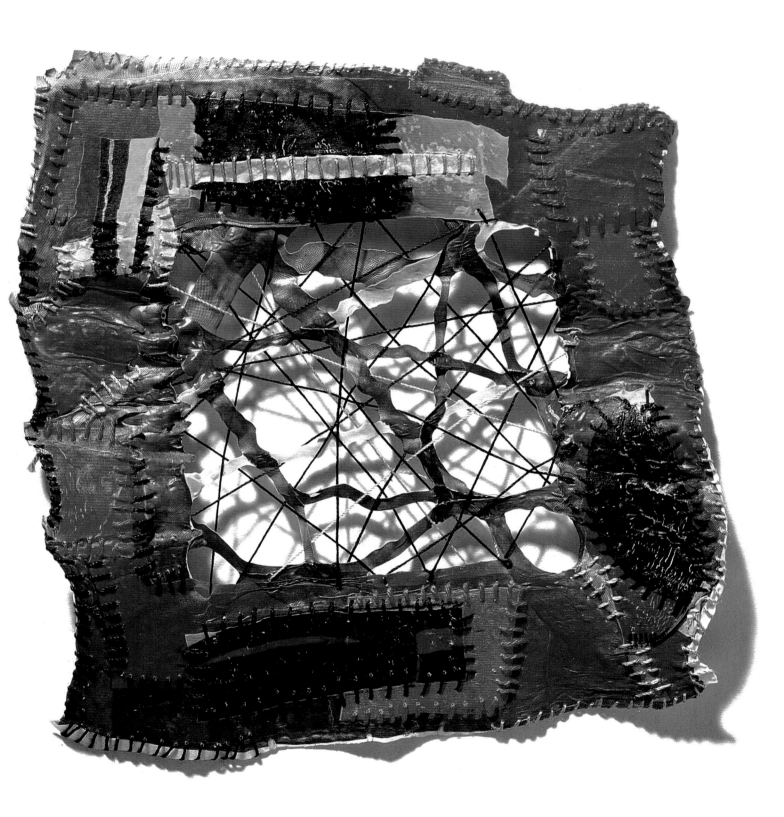

SUSPENDING

Using strips of polythene as anchoring points, it is possible to create small pieces that hang within a space. The patches can be anchored by just one hanging strip, or by many.

1 The first step is to make a patch with its anchor strips. Prepare a polythene-backed patch – it should have been ironed and completed. The patch may be a disc of stitching, a textured piece of fabric, or any other suitable patch. Lay the patch face down on the parchment.

2 Cut very long, narrow strips of polythene, and place them, in two layers, in any of the positions shown, or any other you choose. Make sure that the strips are at least two or three times the required finished length, as they will shrink greatly.

3 Iron as usual, pressing firmly to minimize shrinkage. If the strips shrink too much widthways, it is always possible to add another strip and repeat the ironing.

4 Prepare a window as described on page 55; place it face down, and within it lay the patch, with its anchoring strips also face down. Lay extra strips around the frame to cover the anchor points, and iron as before. Remove the piece from the parchment and trim away any excess anchor strips. The suspended patch and the frame can be further stitched if required.

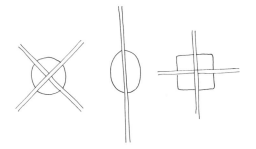

◀ **Fig 40:** Different arrangements of anchor strips

◀ **Fig 41:** Two suspended patches. *Left* Machine-stitched surface and edges. *Right* Hand-sewn with seeding and wrapping, and a border of whipped blanket stitch.

◀◀ **Fig 42:** A net inserted into a window.

Suspending non-polythene patches

It is possible to use an item or patch made of a non-melting material – a button, scrap of fabric, thin wood, paper and so on – but the anchor points must be on both the front and back of the object, so that it is actually contained and held in place by the fused strips. The preliminary stages are therefore different, as follows.

1 Lay strips down in the required arrangement, and place the patch (or other non-fusible object), face up on top.

2 Place a second set of strips over the patch, placing them directly above the first strips, with the patch in between.

3 Cover and iron as before to fuse the strips and contain the patch. Proceed as before to complete the sample.

Alternative method

If your central piece is made of a material that can be pierced with a needle, it is possible to hang it either from a single thread or many finer threads. Just attach the thread or threads to the top of the patch. Lay the patch and window face down, with the thread(s) extending well beyond the frame. Where the thread(s) cross the back of the window frame, cover them with strips of polythene and fuse these into position by ironing as usual. You can cut the threads level with the frame, or finish off with a bead.

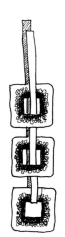
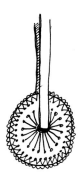

▲ Fig 43:
Suspending non-polythene patches.

▼ Fig 44:
Three suspension methods.

WEAVING STRIPS

Weaving strips in and out of each other offers great scope for creating pieces with a regular structure or repetitive rhythm. Depending on how closely together the polythene strips are woven, a piece may appear solid or may have gaps and holes. The weaving will produce a two-layered piece, but if you wish to stitch further into it, it is advisable to lay the weaving on a base of polythene, so that you ultimately have three layers.

Remember that warp threads run from bottom to top, and weft from right to left.

Regular chequer board squares

1 Take a piece of blue polythene, about 10 x 15 cm (4 x 6 inch) or preferred size, and cut vertical strips approximately 1 cm (1/2 in) wide, to within 1 cm (1/2 in) of the top and bottom of the piece. Place it on a base of polythene of the same size as the first piece, with some baking parchment beneath it.

2 Cut a series of red stripes 1 cm (1/2 in) wide, and weave them into the blue warp strips, pushing the strips up to touch the row above, so that no gaps are left in the weaving – unless you require some gaps and holes as part of your design.

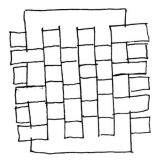

3 Cut squares of gold sequin waste and position them at regular intervals. Place baking parchment over the top and iron firmly to fuse.

4 Cut these into 9-patch (or more) pieces, with the gold in the centres.

5 Place these patches on a matching ground fabric and sew in position with gold thread, using bold hand stitches around the edges to emphasize the squares. Thread a fine gold cord beneath these stitches to give further emphasis. Any other stitching should be very simple, keeping to the regular checked effect.

This regular weaving gives a formal structure to the piece, but other effects are easily achieved by varying the areas and shapes within the woven piece, or by varying the shapes and sizes of the weaving strips, as described below.

Further ideas

- Vary the colours of the warp, using individually cut strips of polythene, which you may need to tape along the top edge for ease of weaving.
- Weave very thin strips in and out, on top of the already woven piece. Weave threads and gift ribbons in with the strips.
- Lay larger shapes on top of the weaving before fusing, to produce areas of solid colour.

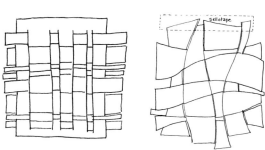

◀ **Fig 45:** Alternative warp and weft arrangements.

◀ **Fig 46:** Woven strips with sequin waste.

CLING FILM (PLASTIC WRAP)

▶ **Fig 47:** Two pieces of cling film were coloured with crayons, and put face to face, enclosing long fine threads. The sandwich was placed between two sheets of baking parchment and heated with an iron. The sample with short lengths of heavier threads had four layers altogether, giving it a greater depth of colour, and a stronger surface for stitch. The small patched sample was coloured as before, and squares from a polythene bag were trapped between the layers of cling film. .

Cling film (plastic wrap), normally used as a food covering, is a stretchy pliable plastic that can provide shiny surfaces for stitch when you require something that will remain malleable and soft after heating. It is more difficult to handle than polythene because of its clinging properties, and needs to be used in at least two layers. It shrinks, but stays flat when heated, and is ideal for trapping and enclosing fine threads, snippets of fabric or papers, paints and shavings of wax. It can be coloured by crayoning directly on the surface with soft wax crayons, which will melt when heated.

For heating cling film you will require the same basic tools and materials as for polythene.

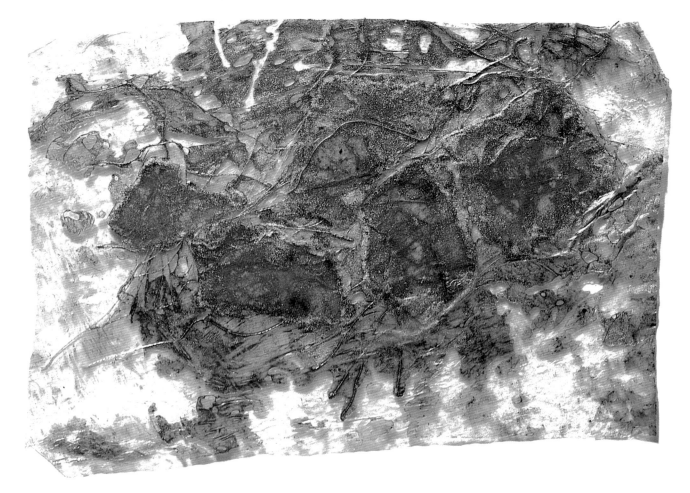

◀◀ ▼ **Fig 48:** A fused sandwich of grated wax crayons, paper patches and threads.

◀ **Fig 49:** Sewn to emphasize trapped threads and wrinkles in the fused film.

▶▶ **Fig 50:** A sandwich of papers and threads was fused, then placed on Stitch 'n' tear, before stitching to emphasize the patches.

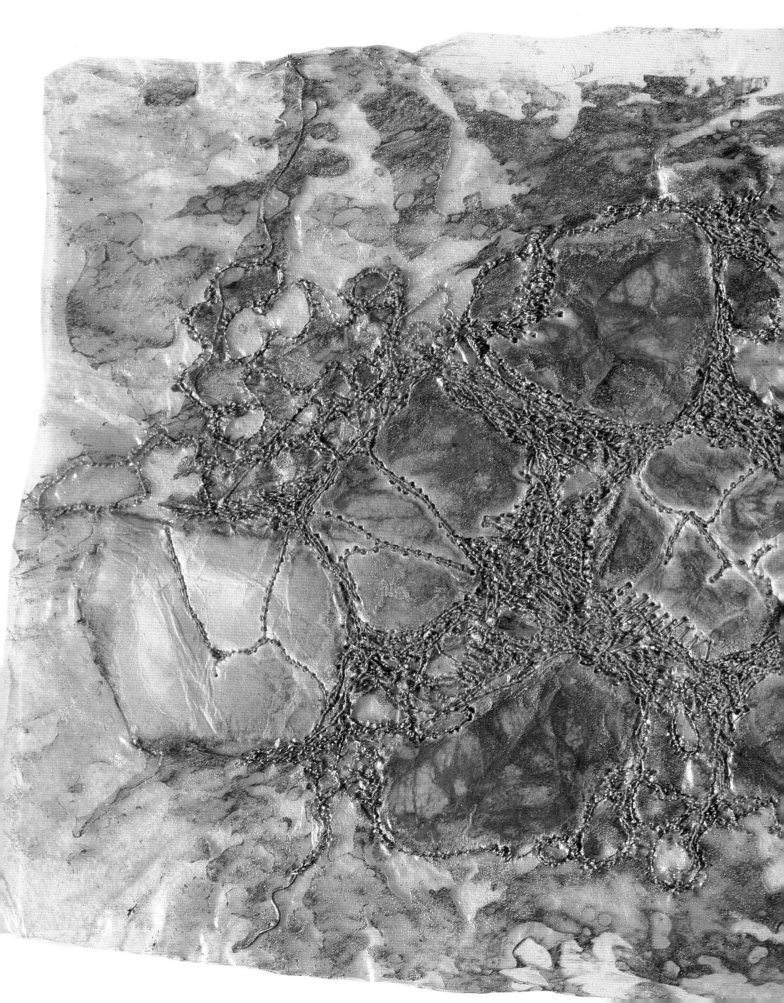

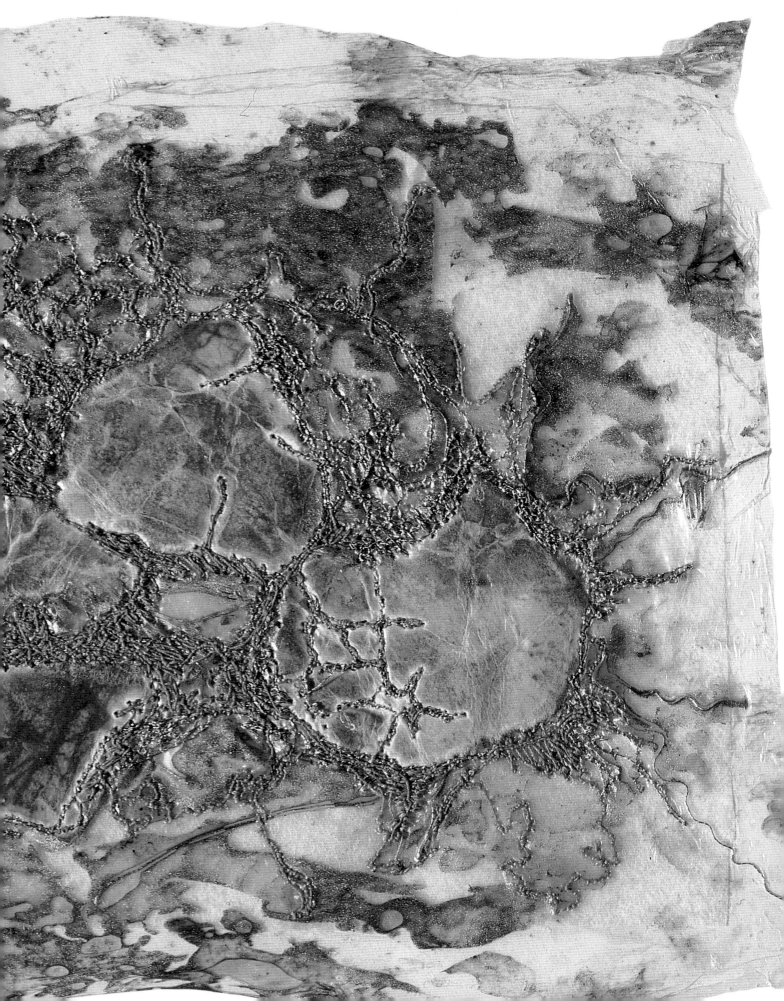

CLEAR FILE POCKETS

File pockets in flexible plastic are cheap and readily available. They are strong enough to withstand stitching, and can be used to create smaller sealed pockets of any shape or size, which can contain a variety of fillings. File pockets come in different weights and different degrees of transparency, and each will provide two A4-sized pieces of flexible film to work with.

Remember that when stitched through the clear areas the bobbin thread will be as visible as the top thread. The needle will make a white mark in the plastic, so if you overshoot the mark with your stitching, any unpicking will show. This can be a problem if you are working on a design with clearly defined shapes. Do not try to bond on to the surface, as it will distort and shrink with heat.

THREAD PARCELS

Requirement

- A file pocket
- A selection of heavy threads
- 2 small flat beads or similar small objects
- Gold hand-stitching thread
- Gold machine thread (or other)
- Basic sewing kit
- Sewing machine

Method

1   Select thread for your first winding. Two threads, similar in colour, give an interesting coloured-spiral effect when wound. The length of the threads will depend on the thickness and on how big a parcel you want – try several sizes before embarking upon stitching.

2   Holding the two threads together, wind them round your index finger, piling the threads up on top of each other, so that when you take the thread ring from your finger, you can flatten it in to a round disc. Slide the disc down inside the file pocket towards the corner seams, remembering to leave a border of about 5 cm (2 in) next to the seams of the file pocket.

3   Holding the sandwich down firmly, with gold thread (or other preferred colour) in the machine, free-machine around the disc in a circle. Try not to stitch into the thread itself, but around the outside of it. Your machine line is not likely to be a perfect circle, but this will not matter – loose lines and irregularity are the nature of the piece.

4   Take your second pair of coloured threads and wind them in the same way as before, then place the wound disc next to the first one in the file pocket, leaving a small gap of about 5 mm ($^{1}/_{4}$ in) between them. Sew as before.

5   Continue in this way, changing the thread colours, and placing the discs in a block of nine. Sew a line around the block to create a square (it will not be a regular, perfect square).

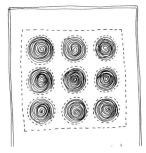

6   Now stitch round the discs several times, before filling in the spaces between them. Use a scribbling motion, going round and round, so that the direction of your stitching echoes the movement of the thread in the parcels.

▶ **Fig. 52:**
Dried flowers, seeds
and tree bark were
sewn into sections
by machine, then
hand-stitched with
fine thread.

7 Cut the excess plastic away from the outside, cutting close up to the outside of the stitched square, then stitch repeatedly over the edges, to enclose them.

At this point, it is useful to hold the piece up to the light, to check for an even distribution of stitching amongst the thread circles. Adjust any areas of scant stitching.

8 Position the flat beads in between the discs, and attach them with a decorative gold thread, using lazy daisy stitch. Finally, sew a small cross in the centre of each of the thread discs. This will not only anchor the centres of the circles, but will enhance the design, since it will be different in scale to the stitches which hold down the flat beads.

Further ideas

- Vary the surface effect ,using different colour in the bobbin, remembering that it will show through.

- Consider what else you could put in the parcels – beads and sequins, ruched fabrics, pieces of embroidered cloth, dried flowers and seeds, found objects and so on.

- Change the shapes of the parcels to square, rectangular, triangular or irregular.

- Consider how else you could anchor the centre of each circle – beads, French knots and so on.

- In between the discs, you might like to use clusters of small beads, pieces of metal, bullion knots in bright threads or couched plastic discs.

Table plastic

A transparent plastic covering for tables is available from large department stores in a variety of weights. The light-to-medium weight is very useful for making sewn parcels of any kind. It is thicker and stronger than file sleeves and is ideal for making practical items, such as a stitching store (see page 127), or anything else that needs a more robust quality.

STENCIL FILM & PLASTIC FABRIC

Stencil film is a clear polyester film used for cutting stencils. It is non-toxic and can safely be used with a soldering iron or a wood-burning tool, without danger of fumes. It can be 'drawn into' with the soldering iron, and fuses easily with synthetic fabrics.

Melting and fusing – basic requirements

For all melting and fusing procedures you will need the items listed below:

- A heat-resistant surface, such as a sheet of glass, well taped around the edges, or a ceramic tile
- A soldering iron with a very fine tip (the Antax 0.12 mm is ideal), or a stencil cutter.
- A wood-burning tool, for patterns
- Fabrics and threads that are synthetic and meltable
- A wad of wire wool for wiping and cleaning the iron tip
- A metal safety ruler and a protective mask

LAMINATED LAYERS

Requirements

- Piece of acrylic or polyester felt, approximately 15 x 8 cm (6 x 3 in)
- Snippets of sheer synthetic fabrics
- Metallic sewing threads
- Basic sewing kit
- Clear polyester film, the same size as the felt

1 Prop the soldering iron securely on its stand and leave it to heat up. Meanwhile, lay the felt on the glass, and lay the snippets of fabric on top to cover the surface, overlapping them to give interesting colour blends, and variations in tone.

Lay a few threads on top if desired. Place the clear polyester film on top of the fabrics.

2 When the iron is hot, hold the work down securely and, using your ruler, draw marks into it with the soldering iron. Hold the iron upright, and move slowly along the ruler, pressing gently downwards, so that the film melts through the snippets and into the felt beneath them. They will fuse together as they melt. Do not press too hard, or you will go right through to the glass and cut shapes from the piece.

3 Work straight stitches into the grooves and also on to the unmarked film, if wished.

Further ideas

- Instead of snippets of fabric, use scraps of synthetic lace, or lengths of polyester thread.
- Make holes right through, by pressing downwards and staying on the same spot for a few seconds. Work the iron round gently in a circular movement to enlarge the holes.

HAZARD ALERT! Wear a mask in case of fumes caused by heat fusing.

▼ **Fig 53:** Laminated layers. Margaret Beal

▶ **Fig 54:**
Enclosed patches.
Margaret Beal

ENCLOSED PATCHES

1 Using a pen, mark out the patches to be cut, drawing directly on the film. Go over the design lines with the soldering iron. Use the metal safety ruler with the iron, just as you would use a pencil and ruler. Hold the ruler down on the surface of the piece and move the iron very slowly along its edge, so that it penetrates all layers right through to the glass.

2 Sew the patches on to a piece of felt, slightly larger than the required finished size, choosing stitches to complement the incised marks on the surface – straight stitches in the sample shown here. Allow the stitches to go over the edges of the patches, so that they become part of the background.

3 Cut a piece of clear film to match the size of the stitched piece and place the film over the work. Using the metal ruler, 'draw' a line around the outside with the iron, to trim and seal the felt and the film.

4 Pierce holes with the iron at regular intervals, using the ruler as a guide and placing the holes just inside the edge. Now stitch through the pierced holes around the edge to produce a stitched border.

Stitched layers

Instead of fusing the layers with the soldering iron, stitch randomly over the work, using straight stitch, zigzag or even a pattern stitch. Remember to use a polyester-based thread which will melt, both on the top and in the bobbin.

This piece can now be cut into shapes using a metal ruler, as before, or indeed any template

made of metal (this technique can provide a good use for old brooches and similar items).

Making a toothed edge

Place a ruler just inside the edge of the piece, positioning it according to the depth of border required. Very slowly, either move the iron from the outside, working towards the ruler, or work from the ruler to the outside of the piece. Practise on a scrap piece to discover which you find easier and which finish you prefer.

Further ideas

- Build up layers of patches, fusing one to the other by piercing through with the iron.
- Melt holes by piercing through the fabric(s) with the iron, and use them for stitching when building up layers.
- Use the toothed edges as thread guides for wrapping a piece.

◄ **Fig 55:**
Three patches of work, including a toothed edged piece, layered and beaded. Margaret Beal

▼ **Fig 56:**
Shapes cut out, and toothed edges. Margaret Beal

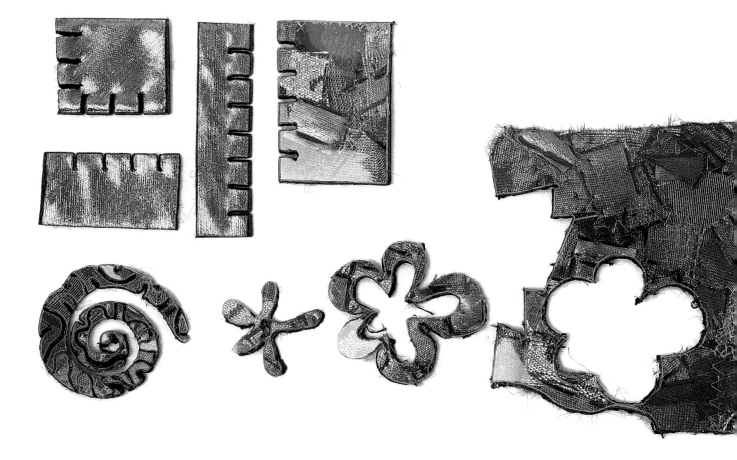

69

▾ **Fig 57:**
Marks made using a ruler (top) and drawing freehand (bottom).

▸▸ **Fig 58:**
A selection of plastic fabrics.

PLASTIC FABRICS

Plastic-coated fabrics, of the type used for raincoats or for theatrical purposes, are wonderful to use with a soldering iron or wood-burning tool. If combined with other materials, such as acrylic or polyester felt, shot organzas, and other synthetic materials, they can simultaneously be cut and fused together, offering possibilities for both linear work and textural effects.

Drawing with the iron

These patches are created entirely without stitching, and rely solely upon the soldering iron for marking and pattern.

Requirements

- Two colours of plastic-coated fabric
- Felt for base
- Metal safety ruler
- Design or motif

1 Lay the felt on a glass sheet and cover it with a piece of the plastic fabric. Cut squares (or other shapes) from the fabric of the second colour, and place them on top. Remember to allow enough space between the patches for cutting out. Make the patches one by one, as follows.

2 Holding each patch down, and being very careful not to burn your fingers, fuse the layers together with a series of small regular marks, rather like oversewing around the edges of the patch. Use a ruler if you want the marks to be absolutely regular.

3 Inside these marks, make a row of small holes by pressing down through the layers, right through to the glass.

4 Holding the iron vertically, move it slowly and evenly to draw your small motif or a simple design at the centre of the patch.

5 Using a metal safety ruler, cut out each patch as before. Tooth the edges as described on page 68.

Using a ruler

One way of creating interesting linear patterns on a fabric is to mark out lines that cross, either at regular intervals or at random. The resulting pattern can be used in its entirety or the fabric can be cut into other shapes for further fusing to other similar surfaces.

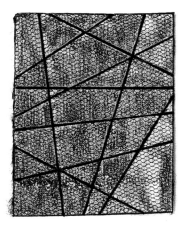

MELTING PATTERNS

In addition to the usual working materials for melting and fusing, you will need a wood-burning iron with a patterned tip.

DELICATE SANDWICH

Requirements

- Plastic-coated fabric
- Clear polyester film
- Baking parchment
- Soldering iron
- Wood-burning iron with a patterned end
- Metal safety ruler
- Hand-stitching thread

1 Heat both the woodburning iron and the soldering iron, and meanwhile place the baking parchment on the glass and the fabric on top of it. Melt through the fabric with the soldering iron, until you have the required degree of disintegration.

2 Cut two pieces of film large enough to enclose the fabric piece, and place the fabric piece between them. Using a metal ruler, and the hot soldering iron, fuse a line all around the edges to seal the parcel. Pierce a line of tiny holes all around the outside, just in from the edge. Use the ruler to keep the line straight.

3 Using the finest of threads, in a colour to complement the trapped fabric, sew through the holes to secure the edge and give a delicate stitched border.

▸ **Fig 58:** Delicate sandwich (right). A lacy sandwich (left) was cut with the soldering iron and pierced randomly all over the surface.

▸▸ **Fig 59 (top):** The patches on the left show a single layer of melted fabric, and a double layer on black felt, before stitching. On the right, similar patches have been machine stitched – one heavily, the other less so.

▸▸ **Fig 60 (bottom):** These patches, using copper, bronze and gold foils together with plastic fabrics, are covered with black chiffon, and enriched by hand-stitching, to emphasize the crunchy surface.

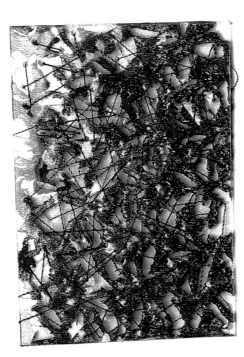

MELTING FOR TEXTURE

Requirements

- Two colours of plastic-coated fabric
- A copper-coloured plastic foil
- Pieces of acrylic felt
- A chiffon scarf – black is usually effective

Method

1   Heat the patterned wood-burning iron, and cut a small piece of plastic-coated fabric – a piece about 5 cm (2 in) square will do. Place the felt on the glass, and the piece of fabric on top. Holding the iron vertically, lightly and briefly press it down on to the surface. Move to another spot and repeat, overlapping pieces, and working at random.

2   Apply the iron for just a quick dab – do not linger, or the fabric may totally disintegrate – but don't worry too much if it does, for you will build on this layer.

3   Take a foil square, slightly smaller than the now-fused fabric one; lay it on the top, and melt again. As the foil disintegrates, you will see glints of colour from the fabric. Some foils fuse better than others. If yours curls and looks delicate, don't worry – all will be well.

4   Take the second plastic fabric, and using a patch smaller than the foil, fuse in the same way. You should have glints of the foil showing through the broken surface. You may continue in this way, using layers of foil and fabric until you have a rich textural surface.

5   The surface may be fragile in places, so cover it with a chiffon scarf, and free-machine in threads that complement the piece. Remember that the more you stitch, the flatter the piece will become. For more pronounced texture, stitch by hand instead of machine.

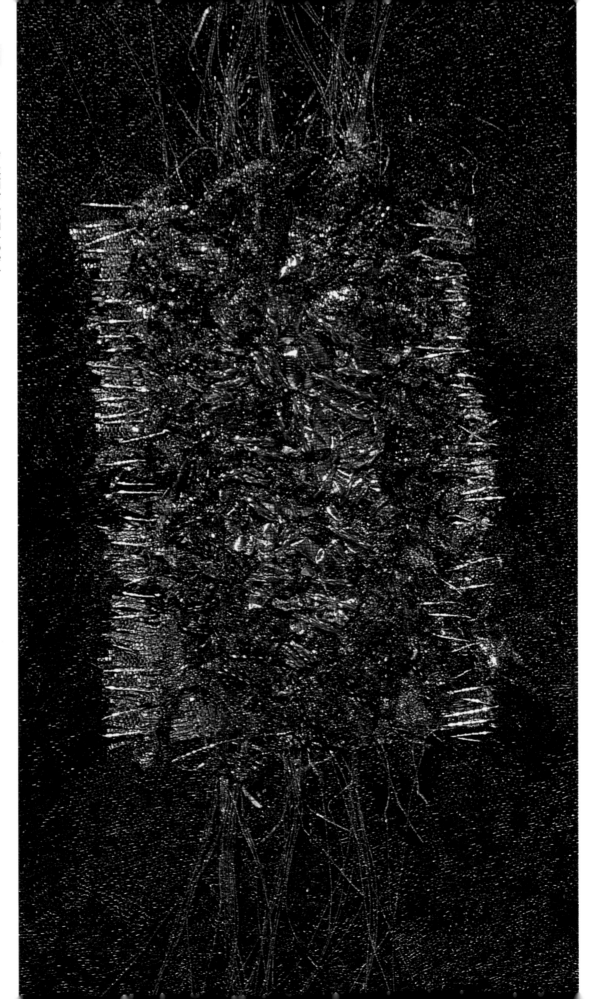

▶ **Fig 61:** Like the patches in Fig 60, these patches, using copper, bronze and gold foils together with plastic fabrics, are covered with black chiffon, and enriched by hand-stitching, to emphasize the crunchy surface.

PUFF PAINTS

Puff paint, often called Dimensional Paint or panda-print, is a water-based medium, which expands with the application of heat. It can be used for stencilling, stippling, painting and printing, and the method of application will partly determine the final textural effect. It gives a somewhat plastic or rubber-like film or coating to the surface of the fabric. Different fabrics accept puff paint in different ways. For fine detailed designs, a smooth fine fabric is advisable. For broken patterns and textures, use a cotton velvet or similar heavy fabric.

After raising, puff paint has a yielding surface, which is easily stitched into. While not strictly necessary, a nylon chiffon scarf, placed over the top of the surface before stitching, gives a particularly good finish, with a fabric rather than rubbery feel to the surface. The following general instructions apply to all the stitched samples.

Basic requirements

- Fabrics to be painted
- Puff paint and water jar
- Colouring materials
- Brushes and stencils or print block
- Iron, ironing pad and parchment or a hot-air tool
- Sewing kit, fabrics and threads
- Chiffon scarf (optional)

Applying puff paint

Always apply the puff paint thinly – you can always add more and reheat, if the results are not as raised as you wish, but too thick a coat results in an unmanageable pile-up when raised. Clean all brushes, stencils and print blocks immediately after use, with water.

Printing

Apply the medium to the surface of the printing block with a brush, with a dabbing movement and not stroking as in painting, since this will push puff paint into the recesses, which is wasteful.

Do not print on a hard surface. Always place the fabric on a print bed – a folded newspaper will do – so that you can rock the block gently when printing, in order to get an even print.

Stippling and stencilling

Use a stiff stencilling brush and apply paint through the stencil with dabbing movements, from directly above and not with brush strokes, which would cause a build-up of paint around the edges of the shape.

Applying the medium with a sponge gives an interesting texture.

Painting

Different brushes will give you different marks, and changes of direction in brush strokes will give interesting movements to the raised piece. Dots and dabs with a fine brush will produce quite different results from broad brush strokes with a coarse hog hair brush.

Spreading

Apply a small amount of puff paint to the fabric, then spread with a piece of thin card, in the same way that you would butter bread. This gives a smooth sheet of material from which it is easy to cut shapes, windows and so on.

Raising the puff paint

Puff paints are best raised immediately after painting, and not when dry.

Using an oven

Preheat an oven to 160°C (325°F/Gas Mark 3). Place the painted fabric on a baking sheet and put it in the oven for from two to three minutes. If the fabric is flimsy and you have a fan-assisted oven, remember to weight the fabric down to prevent it flying around the oven. When the puff paint is fully raised it will be white and opaque.

Make sure that the fabric used will tolerate the heat required. You may need a cooler oven, which will then take longer to raise the puff paint. At 140°C (285°F) you will need approximately 5 minutes of heat.

Using an iron

Dry the surface with a hair dryer for just a few seconds to remove the immediate wetness. Lay the piece, paint side down, on a folded towel or similar thick soft surface.

Place a piece of baking parchment over the piece and, with the iron at its cotton setting, move it steadily and slowly over the entire surface of the work, allowing the heat to penetrate. As the expansion takes place, the fabric will pucker and distort – this is normal, so don't worry.

Lift the parchment frequently to monitor progress. Thicker fabrics, such as velvet, will take longer than thinner ones, such as calico. When the painted area becomes raised, white and opaque, it is then ready to be coloured.

Using a hot-air tool

Place the puff-painted piece, wet side up, on a heat-resistant surface. If the fabric is flimsy, you may need to place a pin in the centre to hold it down. Holding the hot-air tool vertically about 12

cm (4¾ in) above the fabric, direct the hot air on to the painted area, moving steadily across it. The puff paint will expand very quickly as the heat penetrates. When the whole area is white and opaque, it is complete. If it starts to scorch, raise the hot air tool further away (don't worry about the scorch mark as you will be painting over it).

Colouring

You can colour the surface with a variety of colouring agents. Best results are achieved with paints that are slightly thick, such as fabric paints or acrylics, but the general rule is that if the colouring medium sticks to the puff paint, then it can be used. Shoe polish works well, and brown polish can have a leather-like appearance when well buffed.

Make sure that when you paint the surface, you extend the painting past the raised areas and into the ground fabric. It may prove useful to paint some small pieces of fabric at the same time, so that you have compatible materials.

Stitching

Be prepared! After raising and painting, your puff-painted design will probably look coarse and unpromising, with clear definition gone, but be assured that all will be well. This is the initial stage of your work; stitching will redefine your design and many adjustments can be made at this time.

Stitch'n'tear or a similar product may be placed beneath the work to make all free machining easier. This is particularly so in cases where tiny dots of puff paint may have penetrated to the back of some thinner fabrics, making it difficult to move them about easily on the machine bed.

RIDGES AND LINES

Curved regular lines

1 Paint some puff paint on to a piece of strong paper, spreading it evenly with a brush. Take a comb (card cut with a serrated edge is ideal), and inscribe concentric circles into the painted surface by rotating your wrist.

2 Raise the paint by any of the heating methods described, and then paint the entire area. Use two colours to get interesting colour blends, and leave the paper to dry.

3 Place the painted paper on some Stitch'n'Tear backing for ease of sewing. Cover the surface with a nylon chiffon scarf; this will make the paper surface more durable. Sew into the recesses (as opposed to on the ridges) to redefine the curved lines. Change the colour of the top thread to match the colours of the areas to be stitched, and let the direction of the raised lines dictate the direction of your stitching, so that the rhythms of the combing are echoed in the stitching.

4 Finally, stitch carefully over but not through the raised lines – covering them without stitching into them – using a contrasting colour for emphasis.

Further ideas

- Use the comb to draw regular patterns formed from straight lines and zigzag movements.
- Cross hatch with short and long lines to achieve linear texture with dense areas.
- Leave spaces between combings, to vary linear pattern with smooth areas.

◀ **Fig 62:**
Combed curved lines on paper.

▶ **Fig 63:** **Straight random lines**

1 Using the end of a piece of stiff card, about 5 cm (2 in) wide, print lines randomly on cotton velvet (or other preferred cloth), criss-crossing and overlapping. Remember that the thicker the print, the higher the raised line will be. Raise the paint by one of the described heating methods, then colour it to your preference.

2 Make some machine-wrapped cords (see page 138) with threads of matching colours and cut these into short lengths. Secure each end thread with a dab of PVA glue.

3 Using thread to match the colours of the painted piece and the machine cords, stitch the background fabric between and carefully over the raised lines (but not into or through them, as they will flatten), to unify the piece.

4 Using an open zigzag stitch and matching threads, apply the short lengths of cord, placing them alongside and amongst the raised lines, giving another dimension to the piece and adding more surface interest.

Further ideas

• Use a fork to print the lines, making regular groupings or placing the lines in a regular geometric pattern.

• Wrap and apply lengths of cocktail stick as well as cords, creating even greater linear interest.

• Make string print blocks of linear designs and mix these with the straight lines, for a more complex linear design.

◀ **Fig 64:**
This floral design
was printed with an
Indian wood block,
painted, raised and
then stitched in the
recessed areas.
Minimal stitching
was applied to the
raised parts, to
redefine the lines.

▼ ◀ **Fig 65:**
A slightly more
complex stencil was
used here. The
sample
demonstrates clearly
the importance of
drawing with
stitches into the
raised motif. In this
case, the leaves
were stitched to
create veins and
break up an
otherwise large
coarse-looking leaf.

PRINTS AND STENCILS

Ready-made print blocks are simple to use with puff paints. Stencils can easily be cut from thin card or stencil film. Be prepared for the clarity of your print to be destroyed by the raising process. Thin clear lines become blurred, and wide lines of unprinted fabric narrow as the fabric distorts with the heating process. But fear not!

You will redefine the lines and the form during the stitching process. Using the machine needle as a pencil, you can draw back whatever you want, and in whichever colour you like. Remember – your raised print is merely the base for further work.

▼ **Fig.66:**
A very simple stencil
was cut from thin
card, using a craft
knife. It was then
used several times
to create a border
pattern. The
unstitched areas
show how coarse the
design looked
before stitching
redefined the motif.

HOLES AND GAPS

Once you have raised the surface of your puff-painted fabric, the surface fibres of the fabric will have been fused together, creating a non-fraying fabric. This gives scope for cutting windows and holes out of your fabric.

1   Paint the fabric of your choice with puff paint, spread the paint as evenly as possible with a thin piece of card, as if you were buttering bread. Take care to avoid a heavy build up at the edges. Raise the puff paint by your chosen method; colour it, and leave it to dry.

2   Cut holes or windows from the piece – they do not need to be square.

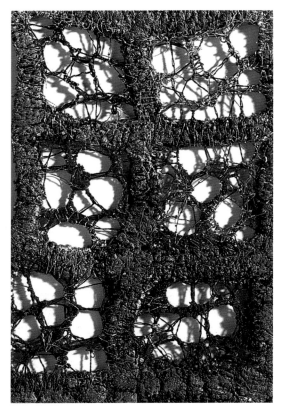

▶ **Fig 67:**
This basic sample is chunky and robust, as it was worked on cotton velvet.

▶▶ **Fig. 68:**
Free-machining was worked in circular windows in painted calico. The piece was then placed on yellow fabric with mirrors stuck in position and sewn in place, after which it was put on another purple piece, and all layers were merged with yellow stitching.

3   Unless you are experienced at sewing across holes, it is best to start with holes no bigger than 2.5 cm (1 in) in any direction. At this stage, do not cut too close to the outer edges of the piece – you will need some fabric to hold on to when stitching.

4   Holding the fabric firmly, with the machine set for free-stitching, begin by stitching across short spans of space – imagine a clock face, and stitch from the 9 across the hole to the 11 or 12, then across to 2 or 3 o'clock and so on, all around the hole. As the lines of stitching cross, they will gradually form a web (see page 140 for detailed, staged instructions).

5   Remember that your bobbin thread will show – this offers some interesting possibilities for colour combinations. Sew smoothly, with no sudden jerks, and at a consistent speed – she who hesitates, snaps the thread!

6   When the web is made, you can work backwards and forwards within it to get a lacelike appearance. Make webs over the other holes, and finally trim the outer border to the required size and embellish it with stitching to match the webs.

Further ideas

- Place the panel on another surface, so that colours show through the lacework.
- Hand stitch into the lacework, darning with interesting threads, or fabric strips.
- Add very small beads to areas of the lacework.
- Couch some very fine wire in place and manipulate it to create a three-dimensional form.

81

TEXTURES

Depending on how the puff paint is applied, it is possible to obtain simple or complex areas of texture, which may be rough, ridged or knobbly.

Brush strokes

1   Using a coarse brush, apply the puff paint to the fabric – in this case, calico. Paint fairly liberally, keeping the brush strokes to simple direct curves, one next to another, and changing direction frequently. You will see the marks of the coarse brush in the wet surface.

2   Raise by any of the methods described, then colour the raised surface, remembering to extend the colour out into the plain fabric, beyond the puffed areas. It is a good idea to use two colours and to blend them to create a third.

Adding stitchery

3   There could well be some areas of unexpectedly high texture. If so, lay a chiffon scarf on top before stitching. This will protect the high points during sewing, and give greater durability to the finished piece. Pin the chiffon around the edge of the piece, to hold it in place during stitching. Put some Stitch'n'tear or a similar product beneath the painted fabric to stabilize it for stitching.

4   With the machine in free mode, stitch into the recesses of the work. Follow the direction of the brush lines, emphasizing the design, and change the colour of the thread as the colour of the surface changes. Think of the needle as a colouring pencil, and colour in your background, before tackling the foreground.

5   Stitching on the actual brush marks, or foreground, should be kept to a minimum, to avoid flattening the lines and to keep them as the main feature of the work. Let the painted colours dictate the colour of the threads that are used. Emphasize any unexpected areas of texture by stitching around them, following the contours of the raised areas.

Stippling

As a method of applying paint, stippling is quite different from the stroking movements used for painting. It is easiest to use a stippling or stencilling brush and apply the paint with a dabbing movement, holding the brush vertically above the area. Stippling can also be done with a sponge. Repeated dabbing gives a pronounced chunky texture, while a light touch gives a delicate raised covering.

◄◄ **Fig 69:**
Coarse brush, thickly spread paint.

◄ **Fig. 70:**
Puff paint was lightly sponge-stippled on a piece of calico. The paint was then raised and painted, and machine whip-stitching was worked in the recesses.

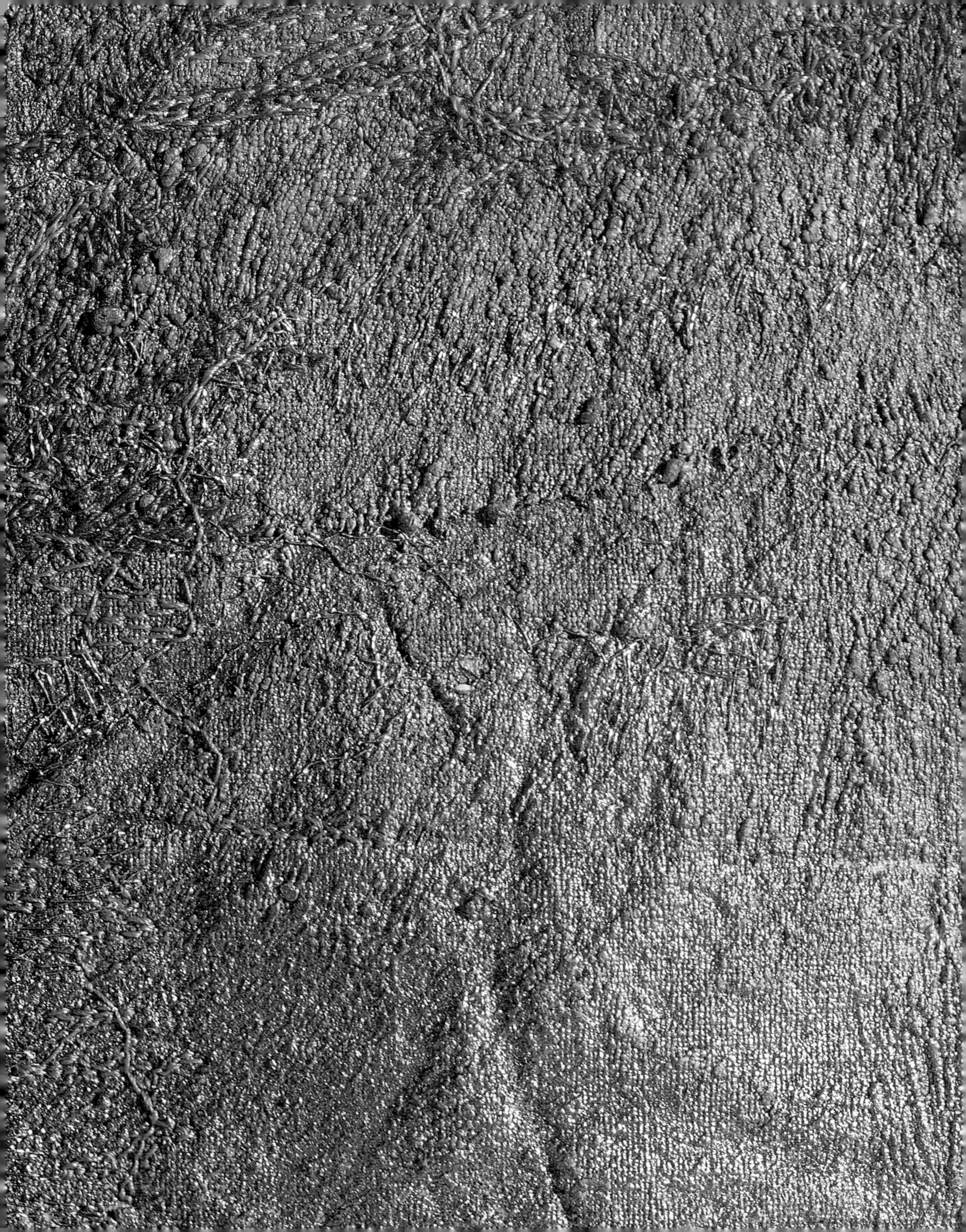

◄◄ **Fig. 71
(pages 84-5):**
A soft brush was
used to work puff
paint well into the
surface of the calico.
The brush strokes
are hardly
discernible, and the
as yet unstitched
areas show gentle
undulations in the
fabric. The stitching
has merely followed
the undulations,
occasionally
echoing a brush
stroke.

MORE COMPLEX TEXTURES WITH TYVEK

You can achieve more complex textures by building up successive layers of raised fabrics, or by applying puff paint to one of the Tyveks before heating it.

1   Paint an A5 sheet of Tyvek (fibrefilm medium weight) with puff paint, using a medium brush and varying the direction of the brush strokes. Apply a thin coat – just enough to be seen on the surface. Using a hot-air tool, apply heat to the wet surface, moving the tool evenly across it.

2   Turn the film over, and repeat. You may well melt holes through the film, but this will not matter. The film will have contorted and shrunk, while the puff paint on the surface will have risen, creating convoluted surfaces with a great sense of dimension.

3   Paint the puff-paint surface, and paint some calico, or any other cloth of your choosing, in the same colours, so that you have a toning ground

fabric. You may like to highlight the peaks of the piece with gold or any other contrasting colour.

4   Apply the piece to the ground cloth with free machining, taking note of the direction of the distortions and sewing to echo them.

If you have holes and melted areas in the piece, you may like to pull it apart further so that you have several distressed areas to apply to the ground fabric.

5   Sew firmly all around the edges, blending them into the ground fabric, so that they are no longer evident, then gradually work your way into the central areas, sewing only into the 'valleys', and changing colour as necessary.

6   Do not be tempted to use a zigzag stitch for the edges as this is a very obvious stitch. It is better to use straight stitch and to colour in, using the needle as a pencil to colour over the edges (see page 137).

Complete the piece with added hand-stitching, to emphasize highlights and to give further texture to the low areas.

▼ **Fig 72:**
Tyvek film painted
with puff paint,
raised, coloured,
then stitched by
hand and machine.

SOFTSCULPT

Softsculpt is a thermoplastic foam which, when briefly heated either in an electric oven or beneath baking parchment with an iron, can be embossed or moulded into another shape. It cools rapidly and retains the new shape, but can be reheated to regain its flatness if the results are not to your liking. It can be painted, then sewn into by machine or hand, and is available in black or white, and in two thicknesses. Generally speaking, the thick Softsculpt is best for small embossed plaques and patches, and to make printing blocks, while the thin version is better for sculptural forms. The following guidelines on heating are relevant to all stitched samples.

HEATING SOFTSCULPT

Using an electric oven

This is the most effective way of heating the foam. Preheat the oven to 150°C (300°F/Gas Mark 2) and place the foam directly on the shelf or, if using very small pieces, on a baking sheet. It will take about 60 to 90 seconds for the foam to become floppy, when it will take on a slightly shiny, smooth and arched appearance. It is now ready to be impressed or moulded. The foam does not retain heat, so is safe to handle.

Using an iron

Set the iron for wool/cotton. Place the foam beneath baking parchment, and iron gently without pressing, moving continuously so as to distribute the heat evenly. After between 60 and 90 seconds of heating, the foam will be soft enough to emboss or mould. Do not let the iron come into direct contact with the foam.

MAKING IMPRESSIONS

When the foam has been heated, it is possible to make impressions in it, either with objects, such as forks, buttons, printing blocks and so on, or by pressing the foam itself firmly on to three-dimensional surfaces, such as moulded picture frames, wicker baskets or a pile of sticks.

The foam cools very quickly and will need reheating after 10 seconds, so it is essential to impress the foam almost immediately you remove it from the heat – the quicker the better.

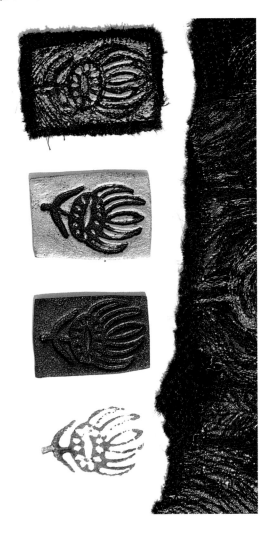

◄ **Fig 73 (from top to bottom):** A print from a block; an impressed patch; a painted patch; a stitched patch.

HAZARD ALERT!
For Softsculpt remember:
- Do not heat above 150°C (320°F)
- Do not use near a naked flame or in a microwave oven
- Do not paint before heating.
- Do not leave unattended whilst heating.
- Do not use with a soldering iron or burning tool.

▶ **Fig 74:**
Embossed numbers
and letters, using a
commercial
printing set.

IMPRESSING WITH A PRINT BLOCK

Requirements

- Print block (or similar indented surface)
- Thick Softsculpt and a pair of scissors
- An electric oven or iron and baking parchment
- Hard working surface

1   Place the print block on the foam and cut around it, so that it is the size of the block. Alternatively, you can cut a circle, rectangle, square or other shape to leave a border around the print. Keep any trimmings, as you can use these to make surface decoration pieces another time.

2   Heat the foam by either of the methods described on page 87 for about 60 to 90 seconds, until it is floppy. Have the printing block close at hand, ready for immediate action.

3   Remove the heated foam, place it on a hard surface, and press the print block very firmly and heavily down into it, slightly rocking it to get an all-over, even pressure.

4   After about 5 to 10 seconds lift the block. The foam should have a recessed negative image of the print block. If you are not satisfied with the position or the print itself, simply reheat the foam as before, and it will rise up for you to try again. If the impression is not clear, then either the foam was not initially warm enough, or you have not impressed it within 4 to 5 seconds of removing it from the heat.

IMPRESSING WITH OBJECTS

Working in the same way as before, try pressing household objects into the foam for some interesting effects. It is often the most unlikely items that give the most effective results, and the kitchen drawer is a treasure trove of very promising items which will create either patterns or texture. Try using some of the following: potato masher, garlic press, spring egg whisk, meat tenderizer, draining spoon, scrubbing brush, stiff nail brush, springs, nuts, bolts, cogs and shells.

◄ **Fig 75:**
Painted papers using a block embossed with a spring egg whisk.

PRESSING ON TO A RAISED SURFACE

This is an excellent way to create unusual textural pieces. Your surface can be anything that is raised sufficiently to leave an impression in the foam. You might like to try some of the following: match sticks, either randomly dropped or arranged, thick string, coarse hessian, buttons, pins, pebbles, marbles, cuboid wooden beads, pasta of all shapes and sizes, and dried peas.

Requirements

- In addition to the previous materials, you will need a flat heavy board or book, and a dish or tray to contain items such as marbles, round beads and split peas.

1 Place your items on a hard work surface, or within a tray if you like, arranging them or dropping them haphazardly as you wish. Cut the foam to size and heat as before, making sure that you have the flat board or book at hand for instant action.

2 Remove the Softsculpt from the heat and very quickly lay it on the raised surface.

3 Place the board on the foam and press very hard for about 5 to 10 seconds, rocking slightly to ensure that even pressure is applied all over the piece.

4 If you are using a tray to hold the items, check that the pressing board is smaller than the tray and will fit inside the edges.

▾ **Fig 76:**
Print block made by pressing foam on to scattered matchsticks.

▸▸ **Fig 77:**
Print block made by pressing foam on to a dish of buttoms.

Fig 79:
Several motifs were
applied to ground
fabrics and heavily
stitched to merge all
the edges.

COLOURING THE IMPRESSED PIECES

Paints used for colouring need to be fairly thick – watery inks and and silk paints will not adhere to the surface. Acrylic-based paints are ideal, as they are thick and remain pliable when dry. Sprays work well, as do some fabric paints. In general, you will discover that some work better than others, so experiment with a variety of paints, and use them in different ways, as suggested below.

- Paint densely, then rub the surface clean, leaving paint in the recesses.
- Paint the surface only, so that the recesses are left plain black or white.
- Paint with several colours, mixing the paints on the foam itself to achieve a richly coloured effect.
- buff with a cloth for a soft sheen.
- Try coloured felt-tipped pens and permanent markers, for controlled surface pattern.

Selecting a ground fabric

Background fabrics for the foam patches should be of an appropriate weight – for instance, they would dominate a fine transparent gauze, but would sit happily on a strong cotton or similar fabric. If the piece is to be used for items such as boxes or book covers, then a robust ground, such as velvet, felt, or craft Vilene with fine fabric bonded to it, is ideal.

Printing with Softsculpt

The impressed patches make ideal printing blocks, so consider printing with the patch on the ground fabric before you stitch it in place. You will get the negative print of the design on your patch, so you know that it will give a sympathetic image. As a temporary measure, it is easy to use double-sided sticky tape to secure the patch to a piece of stiff card, for making a

print block. For permanent use, it is advisable to stick the patch to a wooden block, using strong adhesive. You might like to try some of the following ideas.

- Print in a straightforward block formation, then try rotating the block.
- Repeat the print as a border, then try overlapping and random printing.
- Overprint with a second colour, offsetting prints so that you achieve a ghosting effect.

STITCHING WITH SOFTSCULPT PATCHES

Machine stitching

Softsculpt can safely be machine stitched, since it remains soft and will not damage the needle. You will need to use a backing, as the foam's non-slip properties make it difficult to move the work freely on the machine bed. When using the thick foam, it is necessary to lower the feed dogs and use the darning foot, or no foot at all, sewing slowly and moving the work carefully.

The foam can be stitched just as it is, but it can also be covered with fine chiffon. This not only gives a fabric surface, but also protects the paint finish. The chiffon is simply laid over the patch, and they are both stitched through at the same time. For maximum raised effect, stitch only into the recesses of the impressed patch, in a colour that contrasts with the raised surface.

Hand stitching

The foam can easily be stitched, using a sharp needle and strong thread. You can bed stitches into the foam by pulling hard on each stitch, or they can sit proudly upon the surface. Sticks, wrapped cords, beads and so on can be applied, for added surface decoration.

◄ Fig 80: The central motif was painted gold and placed on a patch of black velvet, then stitched with black into the recesses. The patch was sewn on to repeated layers of gold and black to form a small panel, which was further embellished with hand-stitching and machine-wrapped cocktail sticks.

◄ Fig 81 (left): An unpainted impressed patch was placed on gold paper and hand-stitched with gold into the recesses. This was placed on black velvet and stitched at the edges.

Free and three-dimensional shapes

Softsculpt can be cut into strips, squares, circles and so on, and manipulated to form interesting discs, beads and surface additions.

It is possible to create sculptural forms and vessels that are already covered with fabric and stitching. To do this, simply add a layer of fine fabric to both sides of the thin foam and apply stitches, before heating.

▶ **Fig 82:**
Squares of thin Softsculpt were heated and placed on a firm surface and pinched up to a peak using thumbs and fingers, pressing down on to the surface at the same time. The undersides were painted gold, opened out and hand-stitched on to a ground fabric in a structured arrangement.

▶ **Fig 83:**
Painted rolled strips were woven into a loose grid, then couched to a ground fabric on which a linear design had previously been machine stitched. Further hand-stitching blended the elements together.

▶ **Fig 84:**
Various cut shapes were threaded on a kebab stick, which was then heated. After heating, the shapes were pushed and squeezed together from both ends of the stick. They were then removed from the stick and painted.

A MOULDED VESSEL

Requirements

- Two A4 (8½ x 11 in) sheets of thin Softsculpt, butted together and joined with zigzag stitching, to make an A3 sheet
- 40x 40cm (16 x 16 in) of thin randomly coloured fabric for the main (outer) fabric (it must be able to withstand heat)
- A 25 cm (10 in) square of thin fabric for the lining – coloured cotton voile is ideal
- A ball, apple, tangerine or other similar 'former'
- Oven (preferable) or iron and baking parchment
- Hand-stitching threads – ideally coloured to match the outer fabric
- Sewing machine and basic sewing kit

1 Cut a circle of Softsculpt about 22 cm (9 in) in diameter. Cut circles about 25 cm (10 in) in diameter from the top and lining fabrics. Centre the foam on the lining fabric and centre the outer fabric circle on top of the foam.

2 Stitch freely all over the surface of the three layers in an open vermicelli stitch. Match the top threads to the top fabric, and the bobbin colour to lining fabric – unless you want a contrast. Do not stitch too densely or the mouldability of the piece may be impeded. You will have a foam-filled fabric sandwich.

◀ **Fig 85:**
Pink/blue corded vessel.

3   Machine stitch all around the edge, enclosing the foam.

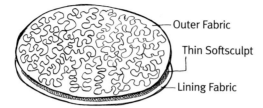

Outer Fabric

Thin Softsculpt

Lining Fabric

4   Cut 1.5 cm (1/2 in) wide strips of the remaining coloured outer fabric. Twist each strip about 5 cm (2 in) at a time, to make a twisted cord, and hand stitch it to the top fabric of the sandwich. Twist as you go, couching the cords down into a very open vermicelli line, to echo the machine-stitching.

5   Oversew the outer edges of the piece, and fill in some areas between the couched cords with running stitch, emphasizing the random nature of the colouring.

6   Heat the oven/iron to the appropriate temperature, and have the mould ready at hand. Heat the stitched foam. It will probably take about 2 minutes, as it takes a little longer for the heat to penetrate the foam through the fabric.

7   Remove the piece from the heat, and lay it face

down on the surface. Remember that metallic fabric and threads retain heat, so use oven gloves if in doubt. Quickly place the mould/former in the centre of the piece, and fold up the outside edges to envelop the former – speed is vital. Slightly pull and stretch the piece as you pull it upwards. Hold it in place in cupped hands, pressing it in shape, for about 15 seconds.

8   Release, and remove the the mould/former. You now have a vessel form, which you can further embellish if you choose.

Remember: if unsatisfactory, you can reheat and re-form.

Further ideas

- Cut a square instead of a circle, so that you have four points at the neck of the vessel.
- Place the former off-centre, so that you have an asymmetrical form.
- Allow the fabric to extend beyond the edges of the foam, so that the top of the vessel has floppy, soft and draping edges.
- At the stitching stage, cut holes through the fabric-covered foam and free machine across the holes to create delicate windows, filled with lacy webs.

MANIPULATED PIECE

Requirements

- A piece of thin Softsculpt
- Scraps of metallic fabrics
- Sewing machine and threads
- Cord or other surface additions
- Either an oven (preferable) or iron and baking parchment

1. Make a Softsculpt sandwich as for a vessel, but use scraps of various fabrics for the top layer. Using a cocktail stick to hold them in place, apply the scraps with a sewing machine, overlapping them. Continue until the entire surface is covered. The sandwich can be any shape. Here, the top layer included metallic fabrics and scraps of lace that had been coloured with fabric paints.

2. You may like to apply cords or further hand-stitching. Whatever you add, make sure that it can safely withstand the heating process. Heat as previously described, monitoring the process carefully.

3. Remove the sandwich from the heat, and place it face up on a surface. Using your whole hand, quickly scrunch up the piece as shown, in order to ripple the surface. Remember that metallics will retain heat, so handle with care. Squeeze the piece together from front to back, rather than pressing downwards. Hold for a few seconds,

then release. The piece should retain its shape. If not, then heat again and retry.

4. You can now embellish the piece further, if required, with stitches, beads and so on.

◀ **Fig 88:**
A manipulated piece.

ADHESIVE WEBBING

Commercially known as Bondaweb, this is a delicate weblike film of adhesive on a non-stick paper backing, and is commonly used for appliqué. The adhesive side is placed on the fabric, and is transferred by ironing the paper side. The backing paper is peeled away when the heat has fused the adhesive to the fabric, which can now be cut and fused to other fabrics, by ironing again. It is the facility to remelt that gives Bondaweb its exciting possibilities for creating interesting surfaces. It is possible to sandwich all sorts of materials between the fine films of adhesive.

THREAD SANDWICHES

Requirements

- Bondaweb, chiffon scarf and chunky threads
- Hot-air tool for distressing (optional)
- Hand-stitching threads in a variety of weights in colours to match the chunky threads
- Basic sewing kit , including a large-eyed needle for heavy thread

1   Place a piece of Bondaweb, paper-side down, on a piece of baking parchment, and place this on an ironing surface. Cut varying lengths of chunky thread and drop them randomly on to the adhesive, so that the surface is well covered. For an extra chunky finish, tie knots in the thread before snipping pieces off.

2   Lay another piece of Bondaweb on the threads, glue side down. Cover this with more parchment and iron gently, pressing down rather than smoothing across the piece. Turn the sandwich over and repeat the process on the other side. Leave to cool for 20 seconds or so, then carefully remove the papers on both sides, peeling the paper back on itself rather than pulling upwards.

3   Place a piece of chiffon scarf on a piece of baking parchment; lay the thread sandwich on top, and then cover it with another piece of chiffon. Place a second piece of baking parchment on top and iron as before, sealing the layers together.

4   Hand stitch the piece, without using a frame, seeding in varying weights of thread using the trapped threads to guide both colour and direction of stitching. The piece will begin to take on dimensions of its own, with an undulating surface.

5   Finally, to give a slight crustiness to the surface and a distressed edge to the piece, pin it on to a board and direct a hot-air tool at the right side of the work. Holding the tool about 15 cm (6 in) away, direct the heat over the surface of the work and all around the edges. The outer fringes of chiffon will very quickly melt, so monitor the process carefully. The chiffon on the surface of the work will also melt, revealing the threads beneath. Beware – the melting happens quickly, so do not go too close to the stitched surface, and do not hover too long over any one spot.

▾ Fig 89:
Multicoloured chunky threads with seeding.

▸▸ Fig. 90:
Bunches of threads were cut into short lengths and fused into a sandwich. The piece was then hand-stitched to echo the lines of the threads. Pamela Richardson.

▶ Fig 91:
Lace sandwich –
partially stitched to
show 'before and
after' stages.

▶ Fig. 92:
Dyed threads and
scraps of cotton
voile were enclosed
in a brown chiffon
sandwich, heavily
machine-stitched,
and then distressed
with a hot-air tool.

▶▶ Fig 93:
Snippets of metallic
fabrics, fused and
sandwiched with
black chiffon, were
seed stitched with
three different
weights of thread.
Beads were then
added to the
surface, after which
it was heated with a
hot-air tool to
disintegrate and
contort the fabric.

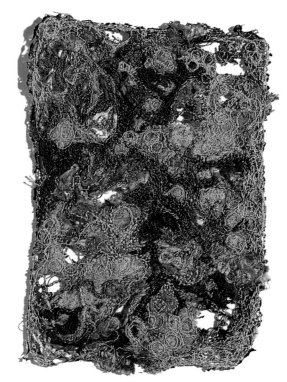

LACE SANDWICHES

Scraps of old lace were used to create a surface with an element of random pattern or design. The scraps were placed in the sandwich. It is only partly worked so as to illustrate the 'before and after' of the stitching process. Hand-stitching echoed the shapes of the lace – the raised areas were oversewn with chunky threads, and finer ones were used to stitch the more delicate areas. At the final stage, the hot-air tool was used to melt the chiffon not only at the edges but also in the gaps between the scraps of lace.

Further ideas

- Trap sequins, metallic threads and fabrics in Bondaweb, then stitch with gold thread for a glitzy look.
- Trap papers, images, feathers or petals from old pot-pourri for an organic look.
- For a more solid appearance, machine stitch instead of or as well as applying hand-stitching.

▶▶ Fig 94:
These three samples feature rippled colour on plain calico, subsequently machine-stitched, rippled colour with no stitching, and rippled colour on a ground of calico to which a variety of coloured fabrics had first been bonded. Patsy Fernandez

▶ Fig 95:
Solid colour on to calico.

FILMS OF COLOUR

Adhesive web is a wonderful means of colouring small areas of cloth. It can be painted, left to dry, and then ironed on to fabric, transferring a film of colour. The consistency of the paint will determine the effects – a watery consistency causes the backing paper to buckle, which creates an attractive rippled effect. For a more solid finish, the paint needs to be thicker, in which case acrylic paints or the thicker fabric paints are ideal.

Materials

- Bondaweb
- Baking parchment
- Iron and ironing surface
- Paints and brush or sponge
- Firm base fabric such as calico or cotton
- Sewing equipment

▼ Fig 96:
This fairground pattern was freely painted and the outline shapes were then retraced with heavy whip stitch.

1 Apply the paint to the glue side of the Bondaweb (this side feels slightly rough), taking care not to rip the adhesive film. You may mix and blend colours and metallic paints directly on the web. Paint right to the edges – unless you require an irregular edging.

2 For a ripple effect, dilute with a small amount of

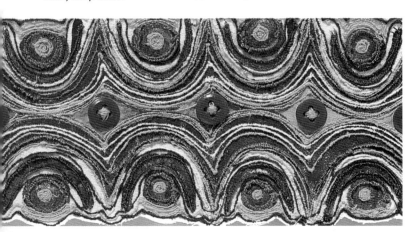

water. For more solid colour, use the paint straight from the tube or pot. When you have finished, set the web aside until the paints have dried thoroughly.

3 Heat the iron to cotton temperature. Place the painted web face down on the calico or cotton, and gently but firmly iron the paper backing, moving the iron all over the surface and allowing time for the heat to penetrate the glue.

4 Leave the fabric to cool for about 20 seconds, then peel away the backing as previously described.

5 Take a toning chiffon scarf, place it over the surface, cover it with baking parchment, and iron again. The film of colour will remelt and adhere to the chiffon, making the surface more durable and more sympathetic to the touch. Apply hand or machine stitching to emphasize the marks and colours.

Precise designs

For bold, flowing lines, patterns and images can be painted freehand directly to the web. If a more precise design is required, it can be drawn out first in the following way.

Draw the image or pattern with a black marker on the paper side of the Bondaweb. Turn the Bondaweb over, and the bold black lines should be clearly visible. Paint the areas of colour, remembering to apply the paint thickly unless you want ripples.

Iron the web to cloth, and then cover with chiffon as previously described.

Further ideas

- Try printing designs on top of the transferred colour, before adding the chiffon layer.
- Lay on extra threads or snippets of scrim or other fine open-weave fabrics before bonding the chiffon on top.

▼ Fig 97: Simple bold brush strokes, transferred to calico and emphasized with dense running stitches.

CUT PATCHES AND STRIPS

When the painted web is dry, cut it into patches and strips. Apply the patches one at a time, peeling off the backing paper before applying the next patch, in order to avoid gaps.

Mix strips and squares, overlapping them to build layers of colour and create an irregular patchwork.

TORN EDGES AND LAYERS

1   Using thickish paint to achieve solid colour, randomly paint a piece of Bondaweb in several colours and leave it to dry.

2   Carefully remove the painted webbing from its backing, and tear it into pieces with soft edges and irregular shapes.

3   Lay the delicate pieces of colour on a fabric backing, overlapping the shapes and moving them around until you have a satisfactory arrangement. Cover with baking parchment and iron. Peel off the paper after 30 seconds.

4   If you plan to stitch minimally, then bond on a chiffon scarf to make the surface durable. If you plan to stitch heavily, you will not need to do this.

Stitch the surface by hand or machine, changing the thread colour frequently, as dictated by the colours of your work.

◄ **Fig 98:**
Above Flakes of Enchantique metallic gold were sprinkled on the web before painting. After the web was ironed to the calico, a few more flakes were added to the coloured surface, which was then ironed again to secure them. *Below* Squares and rectagles applied in a regular manner.

▼ **Fig 99:**
Fragments from a piece of ripple-coloured web with Enchantique gold flakes on the surface were laid down so that the lines ran in different directions, overlapping each other, to give a soft cross-hatched effect, ready for lines of simple hand-stitching.

Further ideas

- Tear pieces of web and bond them to fabric; cover with chiffon, and then use a hot air tool to distress the surface.

- For a really delicate piece, bond a chiffon scarf on to each side of the web.
- Lay scraps of fine fabrics on the surface, matching the colours, to create a collage for stitching.

▲ **Fig 100:**
Partially stitched to show unworked areas of colour.

Chapter Three
Projects

BOOK JACKET

Unlike an embroidered bound book cover, which is a permanent fixture, this cover is transferable from one book to any other of the same size. If your jacket is intended for a book that will eventually be filled with pages, then it is a good idea to start with a book of standard readily-available dimensions.

Requirements

- Book to be covered and a finished stitched piece
- Pelmet Vilene, enough to circle the book one and a half times, with 3 cm (1¼ in) to spare in both length and width
- Ground fabric, the same amount as pelmet Vilene, plus a strip 2 cm (¾ in) deep and twice the width of the book from one cover edge round the spine to the other
- Bondaweb – the same amount as ground fabric
- Craft knife, cutting board and T-square
- Sewing machine with zigzag facility
- PVA glue and cocktail stick
- Basic sewing kit

Measuring and cutting

1 Bond the fabric to the Vilene, making sure that it is wrinkle-free and adheres firmly.
2 Measure the girth of the closed book, from one cover edge round the spine to the other. The tape measure should rest against the book without being pulled too tightly. To this measurement, add an allowance – for a girth of up to 35 cm (14 in), add 12 mm (½ in), and for girths of from 35 to 70 cm (14 to 28 in), add 16 mm (⅔ in).
3 Measure the height of the book and add 12 mm (½ in).
4 The jacket sleeves should measure the height,

as above, and half the width of a cover, plus the same allowances as above. Double check all measurements and write them down.

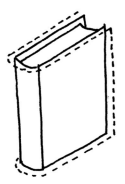 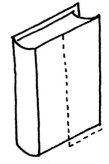

◀◀ **Fig 1:** Black velvet book jacket with gold patch.

◀ **Fig 2:** Girth height and sleeve measurements.

5 Using a T-square to ensure perfect right-angled corners, mark out the book jacket and sleeves on the white side of the bonded Vilene.
6 With a sharp craft knife and a metal safety ruler, cut out the three marked pieces.

Constructing the jacket

7 Wrap the jacket around the book, and draw two lines to mark the position of the spine on the white side, then tack to indicate the position of the spine on the fabric side.
8 On the Vilene side, bond a strip of fabric 2 cm (¾ in) wide at the top and bottom edges of the jacket.
9 Position your embroidered piece on the front cover. Allow a slightly deeper border at the bottom than at the top, or the piece may appear to be set too low – an optical illusion. Tack thoroughly all round the edge and in a grid formation. An optional extra is to position and tack a decorative spine strip or piece on the back cover in the same way.
10 Stitch the embroidered panel (or panels) into place using zigzag or any other type of stitching

which will cover the edges. You can stitch into the centre of the panel to further secure it if desired. You may choose to add cords or braids to the edges of the panels. Any further embellishments must be done at this stage, before the sleeves are joined to the main piece.

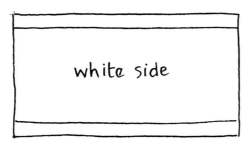

▶ **Fig.3**
Placing of lining strips.

▶▶ **Fig. 7**
Inside of jacket with sleeves sewn into place.

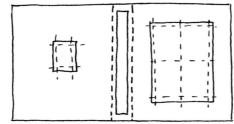

▶ **Fig. 4**
Position of decorative panels.

▼ **Fig. 5:**
Centring the fabric under the foot.
Fig. 6:
Totally enclosing the corner.

Preparing and attaching the sleeves

11 Using a zigzag stitch of medium width and fairly short length – not as closely set as a buttonhole stitch, but close enough to give a good edging – sew around all the edges of each sleeve piece. Make sure that you centre the fabric edge under the foot as shown, so that the needle goes zig into the fabric, and zag outside it, wrapping the edge of the fabric.

Stitch right to the very end of each side and when reaching the corner, stop sewing with the needle on the outside edge of the fabric. As you turn the work and begin to sew the next side, you will sew over the last few stitches of the previously stitched side, thus totally enclosing the corner.

12 In the same manner, sew all round the edges of the jacket body. All three pieces are now ready to assemble.

13 With wrong sides together, place the sleeves on the jacket, and tack carefully in place, matching corners.

14 As before, zigzag stitch all around the edges, starting and finishing at the spine. Sew carefully as you stitch through both the jacket and the sleeves. Again, pay careful attention to the corners, making sure that they are fully enclosed by stitches.

15 Increase your stitch width to 4 or 5 and stitch

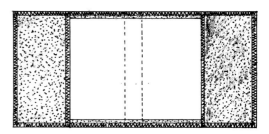

around once more. You may like to change the colour of your thread to give a two-tone effect to the edging. Fold back the covers of the book, ease the jacket in place, stand back and admire!

Tips and hints

Write down all measurements before marking and cutting the fabrics, and double check them before you cut.

If the jacket is too big, it can be reduced in size (height or girth or both) by running a line of straight stitching just inside the zigzag edging. This will ensure a closer fit and also give a lip to the book jacket.

It is slightly trickier to alter the jacket if you find you have made it too small, but there is a solution, as long as the height is the right size. If it is too small in girth, you can cut down the spine of the jacket, using a T-square and craft knife. You can then insert a narrow strip, butting the edges together, and zigzagging across the two joins – it sounds drastic, but it works and can look like an intentional feature.

To protect the corners, apply PVA glue to them with a cocktail stick. Although white on application, the glue will be transparent when dry and will not detract from the appearance of the cover, but the plastic coating will give greater durability to the corners, which will be the areas of heavy wear. Any stray threads can be smoothed down and secured in a similar way.

Variations

- Make a cord with a bead or apply loops to the spine, to act as pen or pencil carriers.
- Consider varying the shape of the edges – they do not have to be straight. At the cutting stage, allow an extra flange and cut shaped edgings, remembering to match up the shapes with the sleeves.
- You might like to singe the outer curve edges with the tip of a soldering iron, to give an aged effect.
  - Instead of using the machine and zigzag stitch, try hand-stitching, using buttonhole stitching with some robust chunky thread, to give a totally different finish.

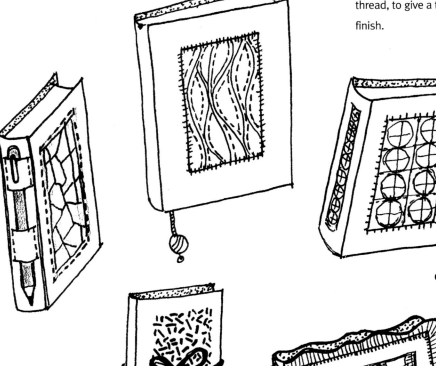

◀ **Fig 8:** Suggested variations.

▶▶ (overleaf) Collection of book jackets. Book jacket, centre back, by Audrey Roche.

A QUICK BOX

This box is not made by traditional techniques. It is a quick all-in-one method, whereby the box is assembled ready-lined, being made in sections using a sewing machine, with the feed dogs up. Each section is a sandwich of two pieces of Vilene – one with the outer fabric bonded to it, and the other with the lining fabric bonded to it. The 'meat' in the sandwich is a piece of stiff card, which is not sewn through during the construction. The box is assembled flat, by machine, and folded into shape, before the final edges are joined by hand. Please read the instructions thoroughly before beginning, to familiarize yourself with the 'sandwich' principle of each box section and the overall construction method.

Requirements

- Stitched piece 12.5 cm (5 in) square or less (but no bigger)
- 30 x 60 cm (12 x 24 in) of outer fabric
- 30 x 60 cm (12 x 24 in) of lining fabric
- 30 x 60 cm (12 x 24 in) of stiff card
- Thin card (cereal box) for templates
- 30 x 120 cm (12 x 48 in) or a 60 cm (24 in) square of pelmet   (heavy craft-weight) Vilene
- 1m (1 yd) of Bondaweb or similar
- Solid glue stick
- Craft knife, cutting board and T-square
- Sewing machine with zigzag facility and sewing kit
- PVA glue and cocktail stick

Cutting the templates

Start by marking and cutting templates from thin card. Use a T-square to ensure perfect right-angled corners, and be sure to measure accurately.

It is very important that you have the 2mm (1/12 in) differential between the lid and the base pieces. Labelling all templates clearly, cut as follows:

- fabric base – 14 cm (5 1/2 in) square
- fabric base side – 14 x 6 cm (5 1/2 x 2 3/8 in)
- fabric lid top – 14.2 cm (5 7/12 in) square
- fabric lid sides – 14.2 x 3.5 cm (5 7/12 x 1 3/8 in)
- card stiffener base 13.2 cm (5 1/8 in) square
- card stiffener base side 13.2 x 5.2 cm (5 1/8 x 2 in)
- card stiffener lid top – 13.4 cm (5 1/4 in) square
- card stiffener lid side – 13.4 x 2.7 cm (5 1/4 x 1 in)

Preparing the box sections

1   Bondaweb the lining fabric firmly to half the Vilene, making sure that it is wrinkle-free and adheres firmly around the edges.

Bond the outer box fabric to the other half of the Vilene.

2   Using the outer fabric templates, mark one base, one lid, four base sides and four lid sides on the Vilene side of the bonded outer fabric. Label the pieces clearly – you can write on the white side, as it will not be seen. Repeat the process with the lining fabric.

3   Now mark the card stiffeners on heavy card. You will need one base and four base sides, one lid and four lid sides. Note that the measurements for these internal stiffening pieces are 8 mm (1/3 in) less than the fabric covered exterior pieces.

4   Check with the T-square that all corners are true right angles and that the lid pieces are 2 mm (1/8 in) larger than the base pieces. Carefully cut out the pieces with a safety ruler and craft knife. Do not cut with scissors, as you will not achieve the line accuracy needed.

Assembling the box base

5   Take the three base pieces (lining, card stiffener and outer fabric) and make a sandwich with the card in the middle and the lining and outer fabrics on the outside. Dab the centre of the card, on both sides, with the adhesive stick to help hold the sandwich together.

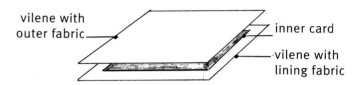

vilene with outer fabric
inner card
vilene with lining fabric

6   With your sewing machine set for automatic stitching (feed dogs up) hold the pieces firmly together and perfectly in line, and sew together, using a wide zigzag stitch (about width 3) that is short in length, but not as closely set as a buttonhole stitch. Start 2 cm (3/4 in) in from a corner, and stitch all around the edge, covering the edges of both layers of Vilene. It may be necessary to go around twice.

Take care when sewing to guide the edge under the centre of the foot, and make sure that corners are fully enclosed (see page 110, steps 11 & 12).

7   Repeat the process to make the base sides, then place the box base, lining side down, and butt one base side up against it. Holding the pieces flat, and tightly up against each other, stitch them together, using the widest zigzag stitch. Do not let one piece ride up and overlap another.

It is important to make sure that the two abutting edges are fed centrally under the foot, so that there is an equal amount of the zigzag either side of the join. This zigzag will form a hinge.

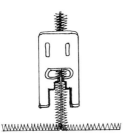

8   Repeat the process to join in the other three base sides. The base is now ready for folding. Place the work outer side down, and fold up the sides to construct the box base.

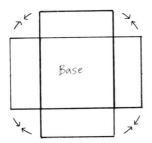

Using a thread to match the edge stitching, hand stitch the now upright box edges, so that the stitches blend in with the zigzag and are not visible. Use a double thread, and start at the top, working down to the corners.

Any slight discrepancies in length, resulting in a small bulge at a corner, can be dealt with by pushing the bulge to the inside of the box with a knitting needle (knitting pin), and sewing firmly on the outside. Such minor adjustments will not show on the finished box.

Assembling the lid

9   Take your stitched panel (any further surface decoration should be applied at this stage). Baste the completed panel to the centre of the outer fabric box lid piece; baste around the edge and vertically and horizontally across the centre. Machine stitch the panel in place, using zigzag or any other decorative stitch that will cover the edge of the panel.

10 Form sandwiches of outer fabric, card and lining, as for the base, and join them in the same way as the base section. If you wish to add a decorative cord around the stitched panel or around the lid edge, do so by hand, using a curved (upholstery) needle.

Fold the sides up and hand stitch in a matching colour, as for the box base. Your box is now complete.

Tip

As a practical measure, use a cocktail stick to spread a little PVA glue thinly over the corners of both lid and base. The white PVA will dry to a transparent finish, so will not spoil the look of the box, but will give greater durability to areas of likely wear. You can also smooth in any loose ends in a similar way.

Variations

Now that you have mastered the principles of this quick, all-in-one method of constructing a box, you will be able to make boxes in all sorts of different sizes and shapes. You might like to try some of the following ideas.

*   A triangular, rectangular, pentagonal or hexagonal box
*   A box with decorated sides as well as top
*   A deep lid which covers the entire sides of the box
*   A lid which is hinged, and secured with a button or tie
*   A tall lidless box – which becomes an open-topped container, with decorated sides

BROOCHES AND PINS

SLEEK AND SHINY BROOCHES

The clear-cut lines and shiny surfaces of your samples of fused and melted polyester films and fabrics lend themselves well to making all sorts of glossy brooches. Although those illustrated here are square, you could make them in all shapes and sizes, and with complex layers and designs upon the surface.

A WRAPPED CENTRE
Requirements

- A glass sheet
- Soldering iron
- Metal safety ruler
- Brooch fastener
- Strong contact adhesive
  (suitable for fabric and metal)
- 4 cm (1¹/₂ in) square of black acrylic felt
- 2 cm (³/₄ in) square of plastic fabric on felt with

▶ **Fig 1:**
Bronze brooch, wrapped centre, beads at edges. Margaret Beal.

ruled lines (see page 70)

- 4 cm (1¹ᐟ² in) square of stitched layers
  (see page 68)
- Threads for wrapping
- Basic sewing kit
- Small toning beads

Method

1 Make a toothed edge (see page 68) on all
   sides of the 4 cm (1¹ᐟ² in) layered square.
   Place the 2 cm (³ᐟ⁴ in) square centrally (or
   otherwise) on the toothed square.

2 Using a thread to complement the colour
   scheme, secure the central square in
   position by wrapping. Begin with a securing
   stitch into the back of the felt, then wrap
   firmly and at random, from side to side and
   top to bottom, using each of the edge slots
   to hold the thread. When you have wrapped
   sufficiently, finish with a securing stitch in
   the felt back.

3 Sew the brooch fastener to the 4 cm (1¹ᐟ² in)
   square of black felt, positioning it a quarter
   of the way down from the top. Instead of
   pinning it square on, you may like to turn
   the brooch 45 degrees so that it looks more
   diamond shape – in which case, position the
   brooch back accordingly.

4 Glue the felt to the back of the brooch with
   strong contact adhesive, suitable for use on
   fabrics.

5 With a thread to match the backing (black in
   this case), and working from the back, sew a
   small bead at the end of each outer slot, for
   decoration. If the beads are small enough,
   they will sink snugly into the grooves. If not,
   as illustrated, they will sit on the surface.

◄ **Fig 2:**
The base square was pierced at regular intervals around the edge and overstitched with copper thread. A square of plastic fabric with a free-hand design was then sewn in place.

◄ **Fig 3:** The edges of a 5 cm (2 in) square of plastic fabric were toothed at very close intervals, and diagonal lines drawn with a ruler. Long triangles were cut from a laminated sheet with a soldering iron. These were then attached with a matching thread. Margaret Beal

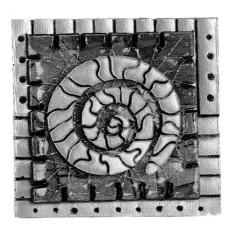

◄ **Fig 4:** A tooth-edged square was wrapped with thread and fused to a larger 5 cm (2 in) square silver plastic fabric that had been previously marked with lines. Finally, a cut spiral of laminated fabric was sewn centrally upon it. Margaret Beal

TEXTURED AND MATT BROOCHES

Small pieces of heat-treated Tyvek fabric give wonderfully gnarled and distorted shapes, with matt texture, and condensed areas of colour. Wire was incorporated into the piece used for this brooch, offering a further possibility for manipulating and reshaping, and Tyvek pieces can easily be sewn into layers, for added three-dimensional effects.

A WIRED CENTRE

Requirements

- A piece of Tyvek fabric in two or three colours for the brooch base, already heated and shrunk
- More Tyvek fabric, painted in colours to match the base piece, but unheated
- Felt to match the size of the base piece
- Hand-stitching threads to match the Tyvek
- Fine wire and brooch fasteners
- Strong contact adhesive (suitable for fabric and metal)

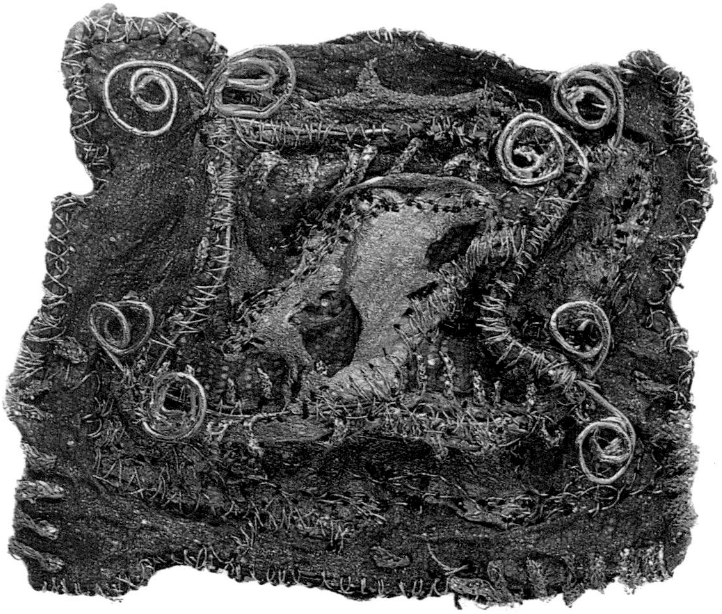

▼ **Fig 5:** Wired brooch. Margaret Lappin

▶ **Fig 6**: Diagram of wires for the wired brooch (centre).

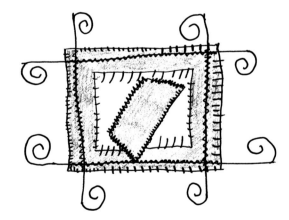

- Sewing machine and threads
- Round- or snipe-nosed pliers
- Hot-air tool and a newspaper

Method

1 Cut the worked piece of Tyvek to the required size, and hand stitch all around the edge. You can vary the thread colour to give interest.

2 Take the unworked painted Tyvek and, using the three colours, make a stitched piece a bit bigger than the worked base – remember that the fabric is going to shrink appreciably. Hand stitch patches of one colour on to another, using a bold thread, and sew around the edge of the patch. Decorate with further random stitching by hand or machine if desired.

3 Lay fine wires just inside the edges, allowing them to extend beyond the piece. Machine them into place, using a narrow zigzag stitch, then curl them into spirals with the pliers.

4 With one pin in the centre, pin the piece, colour side up, to a folded newspaper and apply heat with the hot-air tool, moving gently and evenly over the whole surface. Stop when the edges have begun to curl over, then turn the piece over, so that it is colour-side down, and repeat.

5 Turn it back and check that all is well. If you feel that some areas need more heat, then direct the tool nozzle at just that particular area, until you are satisfied. The wires will have distorted and twisted into a new shape, but you can twist them again if you wish.

6 Sew the wired piece to the already marked and stitched backing piece, stitching by hand. Using the piece itself as a template, draw the shape on the felt, and cut it out.

7 Decide which way up your brooch will be, then sew the brooch fastener to the felt shape, a quarter of the way down from the top. Glue the felt to the back of the brooch, using a strong contact adhesive suitable for use with fabrics.

Variations

- Incorporate other plastics, such as sequin waste, that will distort and buckle with heat to give another texture.
- Sew glass beads to the surface, either before heating so that they become bedded into the surface, or afterwards so that they stand proud.
- Layers of Tyvek fabric are painted, machine stitched and beaded, then heated to gnarled irregular shapes. They are then sewn by hand into layered forms.

▼ **Fig 7:**
To make this crusty layered brooch, small long patches of Tyvek fabric were painted in the same colours as a stitched and heated base piece that had already been prepared. Each patch was machine-stitched, and small glass beads were sewn in a small area. The pieces were then heated into gnarled and irregular shapes. In turn, each of the strips was sewn by hand to the one beneath, and the felt and fastening applied as before.
Margaret Lappin

LAPEL PIN

It is very easy to make attractive pins from just a few beads and one of your special wrapped or incised beads. Long pins can be used as lapel pins or hat pins.

Requirements

- A long Tyvek fabric feature bead
- A few gold beads in several sizes, including small spacer beads
- A gold crimp bead
- A 12.5 cm (5 in) brass hat
- pin and clutch
- Snipe-nosed pliers

▸ **Fig 8:** Three lapel pins.

▸▸ **Fig 9:**
Lapel pin bead arrangements.

Method

1   Remove the clutch from the hat pin, and thread on the gold beads. The size of your feature bead will determine the number of additional beads, bearing in mind that the combination must not take up more than half the length of the pin.

2   Thread on the feature bead, making sure that the preceding gold bead is larger than the central hole of the feature bead.

3   Thread two or three more gold beads on to the pin to complete the arrangement. Give consideration to the shape and size of beads, so that you have an interesting outline shape,

4   Finally, push all the beads firmly up to the top, place a gold crimp bead on the pin, and with the snipe-nosed pliers, squash it tightly on to the pin, to hold all the beads in place. Although not strictly necessary, for added security, you may like to place a dab of glue on the inside of the crimp bead before squashing.

Tip

Once you have selected your beads, try several arrangements on the pin before deciding the final order. Do not put beads more than halfway down the length of the pin, or it will look top heavy and will not sit properly when worn on a garment. Flat, disclike spacer beads are very useful for lapel pins and can be combined with other beads to make interesting shapes above and below the main feature bead.

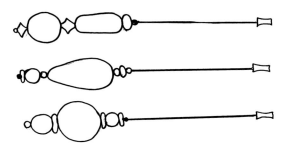

BAR PINS

A hat pin can also be bent and formed with pliers into an attractive bar brooch pin.

Requirements

- A Tyvek fabric feature bead
- A selection of gold beads in various sizes and shape
- A 12.5 cm (5 in) brass hat pin
- Snipe-nosed pliers

Method

1 Using the pliers, bend a 1 cm (1/2 in) length at the head end of the pin, up at a right angle to it.

2 Next, bend about a quarter of it back at a right angle to make a stay.

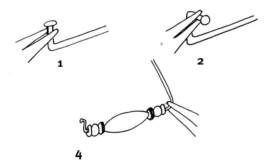

3 Measure the remaining straight length of pin. The beads that you thread on should fill just under half this length. Thread your beads on in the preferred order, remembering to vary the sizes and shapes to give interest to the overall design.

◀ **Fig 10:**
Pin brooches.

4 Double check that the beads do not take up more than half the straight length of the pin. Then, with the pliers next to the last bead, bend the remaining length of pin up at right angles.

5 Use the pliers to bend the upright pin back over the beads, so that the point hooks behind the prepared stay.

123

Projects

CONCERTINA OR TURNABOUT BOOK

This little book has securing cords that are tied in different ways for different openings. With both cords untied, you have a concertina book, while tied on the left the book opens in the usual way. Undo the left, tie on the right, turn the book over and the back becomes the front.

Materials

- Two stitched pieces, each A6 (14.8 x 10.5 cm/5³/⁴ x 4¹/⁸ in) or less, each stitched to a fine fabric backing, measuring 15 x 20 cm (6 x 8 in)
- One A3 (29.6 x 42 cm/11⁵/⁸ x 16¹/² in) sheet of cartridge paper
- Strong glue, such as Copydex
- Double-sided Sellotape (Scotch tape)
- Two pieces of A6 mount board
- Two pieces of heavy paper, also A6
- Two pieces of flat cord or ribbon, each 50 cm (20 in) long
- Craft knife and cutting board

Preparing the covers

1 Place the stitched piece on its fabric base, face down on the table, and centre one of the board pieces over it. Trim just the corners of the fabric, as shown, to within 1 cm (a scant ¹/² in) of the board.

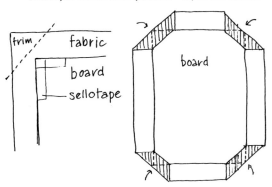

2 Apply double-sided Sellotape to the corners of the board and fold the fabric over as shown, making sure that you fold tightly up to the corner of the board.

3 Apply adhesive all round the edge of the board and over the folded corners, then fold the fabric over, ensuring clean tight edges and neat corners.

4 Knot the ends of one of the flat cords, or thread a bead on each end for decoration, then position the cord across the back of the cover, halfway down. Glue the cord in place and leave it to dry.

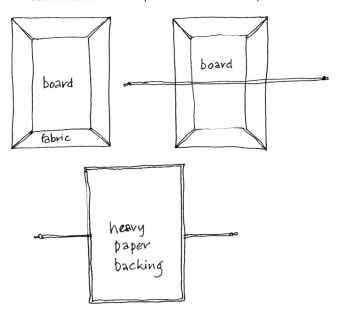

5 Glue a piece of the heavy paper on top of the cord to neaten and secure.

6 Repeat to make the second cover.

Preparing the concertina

7 Using the craft knife, cut the cartridge paper in half lengthways; fold each piece in four and zigzag as shown (overleaf). Glue the two zigzags together, to make one long strip with seven sections.

◀ **Fig 11:**
Books by Della Barrow and Carol Newman

125

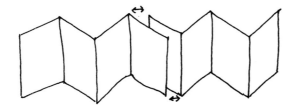

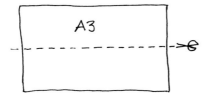

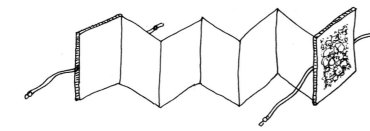

Assembling the book

8   Spread adhesive thinly but thoroughly all over the inside of a cover, paying particular attention to the edges, and join firmly to the end section of the concertina. Repeat the procedure with the other end and the second cover. Fold the concertina and lay it flat, weighted with a heavy book or other weight until dry.

Your book is now ready for filling with samples, photographs or memorabilia.

Variations on a theme

- Make a longer concertina by joining on further sections. Make sure that you end up with an odd number of sections.

- Using the same principles of construction, make books of different proportions – try tall and thin with two sets of ties on each side, and experiment with other shapes.

▶ **Fig 12:** Stitching Store. Celia Litchfield-Dunn

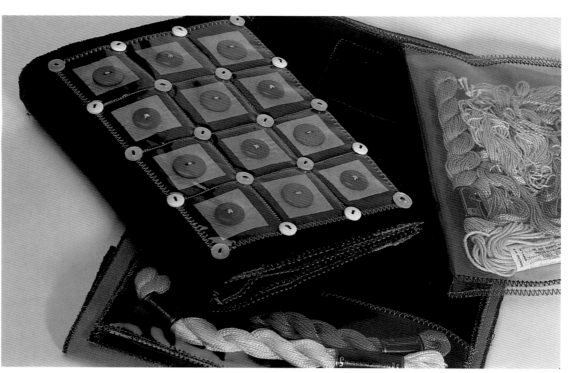

STITCHING STORE

This is a soft fold-round storage system, designed as a handy container for sewing essentials. It has zipped plastic pockets, a removable sewing bag and handy containers for threads, needles and other sewing paraphernalia. The plastic sheet used here is transparent table-covering plastic, available in the home-furnishing departments of large department stores.

Requirements
- A worked panel no bigger than 14 x 18 cm (5¹/₂ x 7 in) for the cover
- 40 x 80 cm (16 x 32 in) of plastic sheet 42 x 47 cm
- (16³/₄ x 18³/₄ in) of heavy felt
- 22 x 45 cm (8⁵/₈ x 18 in) of robust cotton for lining
- 22 x 45 cm (8⁵/₈ x 18 in) of Bondaweb
- 25 cm (10 in) of sew-on Velcro
- Three zips (zippers), each 18 cm (7 in) long
- 15 cm (6 in) of 1 cm (¹/₂ in) wide elastic
- Sewing machine and threads to match/contrast with the felt of front panel
- Craft knife
- Cutting board
- Metal safety ruler
- T-square or quilter's rule
- Marking pens

Double pocket

1   Mark out the pieces A to F on the plastic sheet, according to the measurements in the diagram, using the T-square or quilter's rule for absolute accuracy. Cut the pieces out with a craft knife, and label them clearly.

Plastic Pieces

A   Double Pocket Back
B   Double Pocket Front
C   Top Zip Panel
D   Removable Bag Front
E   Removable Bag Back
F   Sleeve for Felt Page

Felt Pieces

G   Felt Page
H   Store Cover Lining
I   Scissor/Pen Keeper
J   Needle Guard Flap

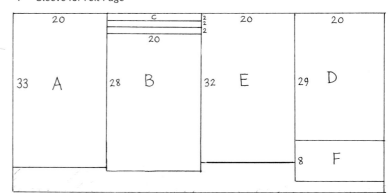

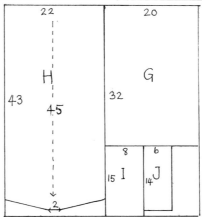

2   To make the double pocket, sew a zip and top panel to a top zip panel (piece C) stitching close to the teeth, then stitch a second line at the outer edge of the zip.

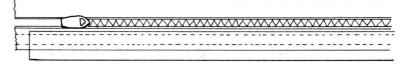

3 Repeat with a second zip (zipper), then sew these in the same manner, one to each end of the double pocket front (piece B), so that the opening tabs are at opposite ends. Measure and draw a line vertically in the centre as shown.

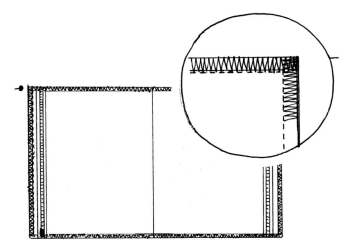

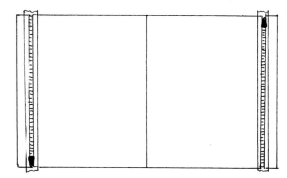

4 Lay the completed section, zip tags up, on top of the double pocket back (piece A), matching edges. Do not worry if the edges are slightly uneven at this stage. Join the two pieces together centrally, straight stitching along the vertical line.

5 Lay the work, still with tags up, flat on the cutting board, and check that all edges are squared and matching. Trim with a craft knife if necessary. Trim zip (zipper) ends.

6 Keeping the work flat, sew the pieces together, straight stitching 3 mm (1/8 in) in from the edge. Sew each of the long sides first, check for square edges, then sew the short sides.

7 Now sew around the edge again, using a zigzag stitch, about length 1–1¹/². Start at the middle of a long side, and make sure that the work is guided centrally under the foot, so that the needle passes once through the plastic, and once outside it, to enclose the edge. When reaching the corner, stop with the needle on the outside of the work, so that as you turn the corner and begin to stitch the next side, you are sewing over the corner for a second time, as shown.

Removable bag

1 Sew the remaining zip to the top panel C as in step 2, above, then join to piece D, to make the bag front.

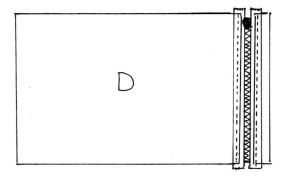

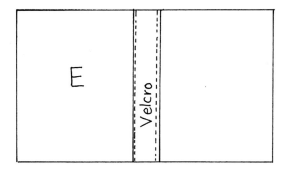

2 On the bag back (piece E) draw two central lines, 2 cm (3/4 in) apart, as shown. Sew the soft half of the Velcro strip in between these two lines.

3 Place this piece, Velcro side down, and lay the bag front, zip (zipper) tag up, on top of it.

Keeping the pieces flat, join them together by sewing across the top, above the zip (zipper) and 3 mm (1/8 in) in from the edge.

4   Lay the work flat on the cutting board and check that all edges match. Trim with a craft knife if necessary. Straight stitch around the other three sides, as described in step 6, above, and then, starting at the centre of a long side, zigzag over the edges, paying attention to the corners.

The felt pages

1   Following the diagram, mark and cut out all felt pieces. It is sometimes difficult to cut felt with a craft knife, as the knife drags. If you have this problem, then use a large pair of very sharp scissors.

2   Take the plastic sleeve, piece F, and zigzag stitch over one long edge. Place it in position on the right-hand side of the felt (double) page, piece G, as shown, and attach with straight stitch around the three outer edges.

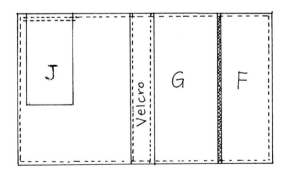

3   Zigzag around the edges of needle flap, piece J, then join it to the felt, level with the top and 2 cm (3/4 in) in from the edge, with two rows of stitching.

4   Mark a channel 2 cm (3/4 in) wide down the centre of the (double) page, and sew the hook

part of the Velcro strip into it.

5   Starting in the centre of the long side, sew with straight stitch 3 mm (1/8 in) inside the edge all around the outside of the felt page, to prevent stretching. Now stitch with zigzag around the out-side of the page, paying attention to the corners as before, to enclose and neaten the edges.

The cover

1   To make the outer cover, lay out the felt cover, piece H, and measure and mark the area for the cover panel. It is important to work with the flap to the left. Centre your stitched panel within the panel area, tack (baste) and then sew it securely in place.

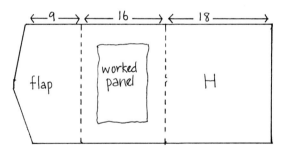

2   For the lining, measure and mark out a lining piece H, and cut it out carefully. This time, it is important to work with the flap to the right of the front of the fabric.

3   Mark out the position of the front and back covers, and mark the central line with a marking pen.

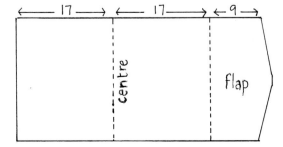

4   Stitch round the edges of scissors/pen keeper (piece I); tack (baste) it into position and sew as shown 1.5 cm (5/8 in) in from the edges. Position the elastic above the pocket – avoid placing it exactly half way up, or it will clash with the position of the Velcro at step 6, below.

5   Stitch the elastic in place, to line up with the pocket channels. The length of your scissors or pens will determine how high you place the elastic – try it out.

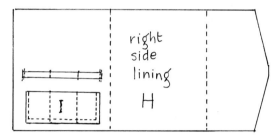

6   Iron Bondaweb to the lining. Lay the outer cover, with the side with the stitched panel face down, and bond the lining piece to it. Zigzag all around the outer edges to enclose them.

7   Stitch a 2.5 cm (1 in) piece of Velcro in place on the lining side of the flap point. Sew the other piece of it to make a closure, centring it on the outside of the back cover.

Assembling

8   Place the cover face down, lining side up, and lay the double pocket section over it, with the zip (zipper) side up, so that the central line of stitching is over the central marking on the lining. Stitch into place with two rows of stitching, one 2 mm (1/12 in) on each side of the marked line.

9   Centre the felt page, Velcro side up, over the pocket section, making sure that it is squarely positioned. Stitch down each side of the Velcro strip to join all three layers.

10 Press the removable bag into place with the Velcro. If you wish, add a decorative button to the outside flap, above the Velcro fastening. Now fill and fatten out your storage wallet with all manner of sewing notions!

Chapter Four
Stitch Reference

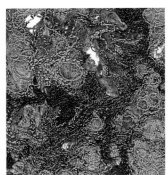

STITCHES

There are literally hundreds of different stitches for the embroiderer to employ, and several comprehensive stitch encyclopedia illustrating them. This section is limited to looking only at the small range of stitches referred to in this book or used to complete the samples.

Stitches can be seen as a means of mark-making, and are used for texture and for added decoration. The most basic stitches, can add colour and tone, emphasize or subdue, blend and merge discordant areas and give definition to outlines.

Remember that whilst primarily used for line, any of these stitches, if worked closely together in a variety of threads or piled up in layers, could be used to create textural areas. However, in this book, a limited range of simple stitches have been employed to fill an area, to blend or to give textural effect.

Straight Stitch

Straight Stitch is the simplest and most versatile of all embroidery stitches. It is a single stitch, but depending on the placement and direction of the next and subsequent stitches, it takes on different names.

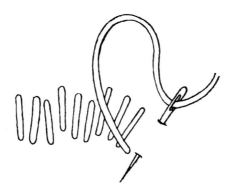

STITCHES FOR LINES AND EDGES

Running Stitch

Lines of stitching can be straight, curved or meandering. Running stitch gives a soft broken line, and the intensity of the line can be changed according to the length of the stitch used.

For a 'hint of a line' make the gaps in between stitches equal to, or slightly longer than the stitches themselves.

For a bold flowing line, the length of the stitches should be greater than the gaps in between them.

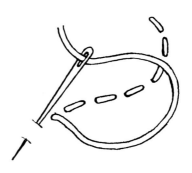

Double Running

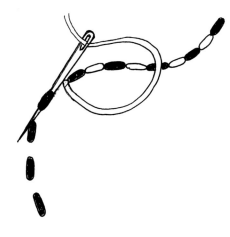

Laced Running

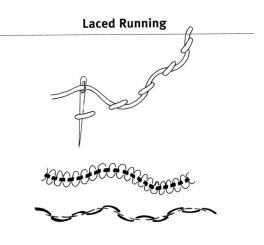

Couching

Couching is a means of securing a thread, cord or other decoration to another surface. The most common couching stitch is straight stitch, but others are effective too.

- Couch strips, squares or irregular shapes of card or paper
- Couch down sticks, knotted fabric strips, and bunches of threads
- Vary the density of your couching stitches

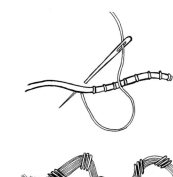

Whipped Running

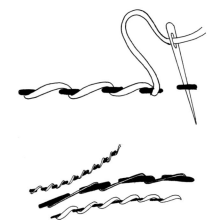

Blanket Stitch

Blanket stitch gives slightly toothed lines, which can be very decorative. Varying the spacing and direction of stitches, and the weight of threads can produce widely differing effects.

- Add beads for a decorative edge
- Overlap rows to build dense lines

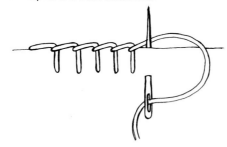

Whipped Blanket & Knotted Blanket

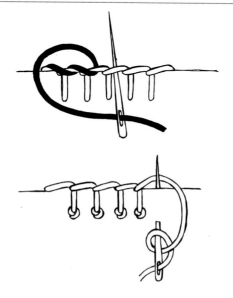

STITCHES FOR TEXTURE AND FILLING

Seeding or Speckling

A most useful stitch that can be used effectively for shading, merging and blending areas, depending on the density of stitching and the thickness of thread used.

- Try working the stitch in blocks for a bolder effect
- Use in 2 colours to soften a line of colour, as shown
- Overlap and work in layers for heavy texture

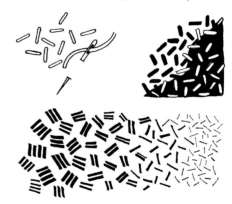

Cross Stitch

This familiar 2-step stitch, if worked untraditionally, can be used to produce interesting random textural effects.

- Use formally for borders. Add beads for emphasis
- Pile up haphazardly to create texture
- Use to couch down buttons, discs and other surface additions

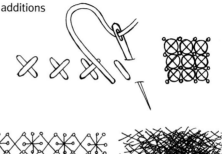

French Knots

These give a 'dotty' effect when worked sparsely or a textured effect when worked densely. They stand proud of the ground fabric and mix well with beads of a similar size to the knot, nestling in well together.

- Give the knot a stalk by elongating the final part of the stitch
- Add a bead (or several) before the final stitch
- Add beads that are bigger than the knot for a different effect

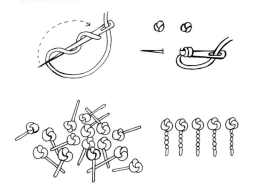

Knotted Stitch

Knotted stitch is a 2-step stitch, the knotted part being worked over a previously worked straight stitch.

- Work with 2 colours of thread through the needle for large variegated knots
- Use narrow ribbons, torn fabric strips or gift tapes as thread for even bigger knots
- Work as a border pattern or as a haphazard overlapping filling stitch

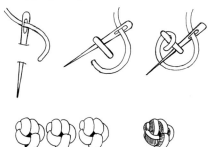

Bullion Stitch

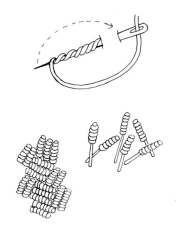

Remember that stitches are often at their most effective when mixed with others. Combinations of various stitch movements whether in formal or informal arrangements, frequently complement each other and add to the overall surface effect.

WRAPPING

Wrapping is a wonderfully useful and versatile technique. All manner of things can be wrapped, from cocktail sticks and lolly sticks to twisted fabric strips, producing fine cords, flat strips and discs, soft ropelike pieces and so on. You can wrap with thread, raffia, strips of paper, fabric, plastics and any flexible material, including soft wire.

Basic Materials for Wrapping

- A core – something to wrap
- Something to wrap with
- A large-eyed blunt needle

Procedure

1 Holding the stick or other core material in your left hand, lay the wrapping thread on it, with the thread end to the left. Holding the end against the stick with the left thumb, start to wrap from the right-hand end of the stick, wrapping away from you, binding the stick firmly.

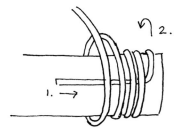

2 Laying each wrapped thread closely against the last one, continue in this way, covering the initial thread end as you go. Keep an even tension.

3 When you reach the last 2 cm (3/4 in), lay the needle on the stick, so that the eye protrudes beyond the end, and the point lies on top of the wrapped section to the right.

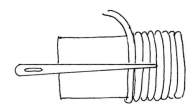

4 Continue wrapping to enclose the needle, until you reach the stick end.

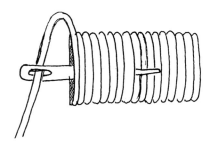

5 Pass the thread through the eye of the needle, and push it to emerge from where the point of the needle already sits.

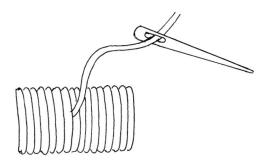

6 Pull the needle right the way through, cut the thread close to the wrapping, then smooth the surface to ease the cut thread out of view.

- Wrap with two or three different threads for a variegated effect
- Space out the wrappings, allowing the core to show through
- Make several areas of wrapping, with spaces in between, and incorporate beads or other things in it, for a highly decorative effect

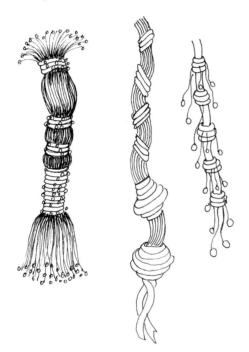

FREE-MACHINE STITCHING

There are numerous books that explore and instruct upon the exciting possibilities of free-machining, but the techniques referred to here are confined to those used in the stitched surfaces, or as suggested developments.

It is all too easy to sit badly hunched up over the sewing machine and such postural problems lead to tenseness, stress, neck ache and disappointing stitching. Be aware of your posture and try to sit in an upright position, with a relaxed approach to work. Hold the work firmly, but avoid stiff arms and 'white knuckle' syndrome! Remember that with the feed dogs down (or covered) and stitch length and width at zero, it is solely your movements that determine the size and direction of the stitches.

- For small sensitive stitches, sew at a fair speed, but move the hoop or fabric slowly
- Conversely, for large stitches, sew slowly and move the fabric quickly
- Move the fabric smoothly and evenly – jerky movements result in broken needles and snapped threads

Colouring in

'Colouring in' as referred to in this book is simply free-machining using straight stitch. Consider the machine needle as a pencil point, and colour in with thread as you would draw and colour with a pencil. Zigzag stitch gives a different sort of colouring in.

Vermicelli Stitch

This is a gently meandering line of straight stitch, wiggling backwards and forwards on itself, which can be worked in lines or randomly to cover an irregular area. It appears as an automatic linear pattern on many up-to-date sewing machines.

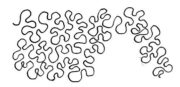

Circular Stitching

This is simply straight stitch, worked in diminishing circles, moving to fill an area. It can also be worked by stitching into a spiral and out again. If worked densely, it can create interesting raised distortions and dips in the ground fabric.

Whip Stitch

This needs a thorough understanding of the tension facilities on the machine, and is worth practice and perseverance. It gives a raised corded line effect, which is achieved through an imbalance between the top and bottom tensions. It is the bobbin colour that is visible, since it comes up and whips or wraps the top thread. The top thread colour will not be seen. The fabric must be very taut, so a hoop is necessary.

1 Fill the bobbin with the colour you wish to be on the surface.

2 Tighten the top tension by a few increments (or loosen the bobbin tension).

3 Bring the bobbin thread through to the surface of the work, and hold as you begin to stitch.

4 Sew at high speed, and move the hoop very slowly.

If the bobbin thread is not whipping the top, then tighten the top tension further (or loosen the bottom). If the top thread is visible beneath the whipping, try moving the hoop more slowly.

An even more pronounced corded effect is achieved if a heavier thread is used on the top of the machine.

Machine-wrapped Cords

This is a wonderfully versatile technique, whereby string, thread, raffia and so on, can be transformed into wrapped cords in a wide variety of finishes. The sewing machine should be in zigzag mode, with a stitch that is wide enough to pass either side of the string or whatever you are wrapping.

* This technique can be worked with the feed dogs up, and a set stitch length, to give an evenly wrapped cord densely wrapped if you have a short stitch length, and sparsely covered if you select a longer length of stitch. The standard presser foot will give a flatter cord.

* For a rounder cord, work in free-machine mode, wherein the darning/embroidery foot will not squash the cord as it is being made.

* Free-machining offers greater scope for creating a wide range of cords, with varying densities of wrapping.

Procedure

1 Select the appropriate width of stitch for the piece of string (or similar) being wrapped, and prepare the machine for sewing.

2 Hold the string with 2 hands, leaving about 15ins gap between them.

3 Keeping the string very taut, place centrally beneath the needle, one hand behind the machine and the other in front.

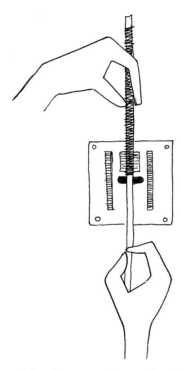

4 Holding the top and bottom threads along with the end of the string, start sewing, beginning about 3 cm (1¼ in) in from the end, moving the string backwards and forwards, keeping it constantly taut. The zigzag stitch should straddle the string, enclosing it.

5 Gradually move along the length of string until it is covered to the required density.

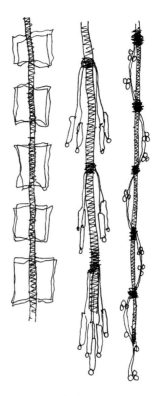

Variations

- Put a different colour in the bobbin to vary the colour effects.

- Move swiftly along the string to give a sparse covering, then repeat several times using a different colour thread, for a multi-coloured cord.

- Lay scraps of fabric and other threads across the string whilst stitching, to get lateral protrusions.

- Insert threads with beads on, so that they hang vertically when the cord is complete.

- Stop and stitch 'on the spot' every so often to achieve large satin stitch blobs, rather like a bouclé effect cord.

Wrapped Edges

Unworked edges of stitched pieces can be easily wrapped with the sewing machine, to give a firm, but soft-edged, and often irregular finish. The piece of work must be moved rhythmically and smoothly, just going over the edge and back again, in a non-jerky movement.

- In free-machining mode, using straight stitch, it is possible to create a random irregular effect, by 'colouring in' across the edge of the piece, varying the angle of the stitching.

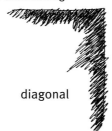

diagonal

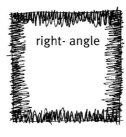

right- angle

cross hatching

- Use different coloured top and bottom threads for interesting colour blends.
- With the machine set on free zigzag, a more obvious edging is achieved. Make sure that the outside edge is actually enclosed by stitch, ensuring that the machine needle passes once through the fabric and once over the edge of it.
- For an even and very regular edging, put the machine into conventional mode, with feed up, and a regulated stitch length and width — again, ensure that the edge is actually enclosed and wrapped.

SEWING ACROSS SPACES

This technique can be a little tricky, but is easily accomplished with patience, practice and self-belief. The important things to remember are:

- Use an embroidery hoop, or hold the fabric very taut.
- Sew at a constant speed without jerking — she who hesitates, snaps the thread!

Procedure

1 Start by sewing around the hole to get the feel of the machine, before launching across a short span of space – from 9 to 11 on a clockface.

2 Continue around the shape as shown until you have a network round the inside edge of the hole.

3 At this stage, you may stitch from thread to thread across the centre of the hole, gradually building a network of threads.

4 Move the fabric from side to side over some of the threads to fill in open areas.

5 Continue building a lacework until you have the amount of filling you require.

6 Complete by sewing over the edges of the hole, and into the surroundings to integrate the lacework Into its surroundings.

start

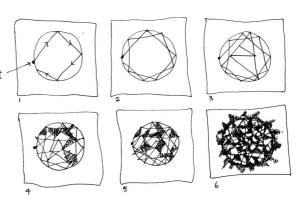

LIST OF SUPPLIERS

UK

Art Van Go
16 Hollybush Lane
Datchworth
Knebworth
Herts SG3 6RE
Tel   01438 814946

Vast range of design and surface decoration materials for
Embroiderers. All-purpose safety masks.

The Bead Shop
43 Neal Street
Covent Garden
London WC2H 9PJ
Tel 020 7240 0931

Vast range of beads, wires and jewellery tools.
Catalogue available.

Fashion 'n' Foil Magic
PO Box 3746
London N2 9DE
Tel   0208 444 1992

Vast range of foils glitters and foiling products.

Fron Isaf
Llanglydwen
Hebron
Whitland
Carms SA34 OJX
 Tel 01994 419523

Complete range of hand-dyed silk threads in all weights.
Silk fibres.

Gillsew
Boundary House
Moor Common
Lane End
Bucks   HP14 3HR
Tel 01494 881886

Wide range of embroidery products, many available in
trial packs. Indian printing blocks.

L & B Embroidery
28 Leigh Road
Andover
Hants SP10 2AP
Tel 01722 336903

Soldering Irons, Polyester stencil film, Polyester felts and
synthetic sheer fabrics, Flat wooden embroidery frames.

Peru 2000
81 Broomfield Road
Coventry CV5 6JY
Tel   07771 747142

Comprehensive range of textile fibres. Inspiration packs.

Rainbow Silks
6 Wheelers Yard
High Street
Great Missenden
Bucks HP16 0AL
Tel   01494 862111

Wide range of embroidery products.

Stamp Addicts

70 East Barnet Road

New Barnet

Herts EN4 8RQ

Tel 020 8449 4892

Enchantique metallic flakes. Hot-air tools.

Strata

Oronsay

Misbourne Avenue

Chalfont St Peter

Bucks

SL9 OPF

Tel 01494 873850

Tyvek (film and fabric), Puff Paint, Softsculpt, Chiffons.

AUSTRALIA

The Thread Studio

6 Smith Street

Perth

Western Australia 6000

Tel 61 8 9227 1561

Range of embroidery and art supplies, Tyvek film and fabric, Softsculpt, Puff Paint.

NEW ZEALAND

Craft Supplies

Diana Parkes

31 Gurney Road

Belmont

Lower Hutt

New Zealand

Tel 04 565 0544

Art craft and embroidery supplies, Puff Paint Tyvek film and fabric, Softsculpt.

FURTHER READING

The Art and Craft of Fabric Decoration

Juliet Bawden

Mitchell Beazley, 1994

The Art of The Needle

Jan Beaney

Century, 1988

Colour on Paper and Fabric

Ruth Issett

B.T. Batsford, 1999

A Complete guide to Creative Embroidery

Jan Beaney and Jean Littlejohn

B.T. Batsford, 1997

Fabric Painting for Embroidery

Valerie Campbell-Harding

B.T. Batsford, 1991

Imagery on Fabric

Jean Ray Laury

C and T Publishing Inc., 1997

Machine Embroidery: Stitch Techniques

Pamela Watts and Valerie Campbell-Harding

B.T. Batsford, 1989

Stitch Magic

Jan Beaney and Jean Littlejohn

B.T. Batsford, 1999

Stitches: New Approaches

Jan Beaney

B.T. Batsford, 1985

INDEX